10 Minute Guide to MS-DOS® 6

Jennifer Flynn

alpha books

A Division of Prentice Hall Computer Publishing

11711 North College Avenue, Carmel, Indiana 46032 USA

For Pat, my sister and one of my best friends.

©1993 by Alpha Books

International Standard Book Number: 1-56761-125-7
Library of Congress Catalog Card Number: 92-75157

96 95 94 93   7 6 5 4 3 2 1

Interpretation of the printing code: the rightmost number of the first series of numbers is the year of the book's printing; the rightmost number of the second series of numbers is the number of the book's printing. For example, a printing code of 93-1 shows that the first printing of the book occurred in 1993.

Publisher: *Marie Butler-Knight*
Associate Publisher: *Lisa A. Bucki*
Acquisitions Manager: *Stephen R. Poland*
Managing Editor: *Elizabeth Keaffaber*
Development Editor: *Faithe Wempen*
Production Editor: *Annalise N. Di Paolo*
Copy Editor: *Barry Childs-Helton*
Cover Designer: *Dan Armstrong*
Designer: *Amy Peppler-Adams*
Indexer: *Jeanne Clark*
Production Team: *Tim Cox, Mark Enochs, Tim Groeling, Phil Kitchel, Tom Loveman, Michael J. Nolan, Carrie Roth, Mary Beth Wakefield, Barbara Webster, Kelli Widdifield*

Special thanks to Kelly Oliver and C. Herbert Feltner for ensuring the technical accuracy of this book.

Screen reproductions in this book were created by means of the program Collage Plus from Inner Media, Inc., Hollis, NH.

Printed in the United States of America

Contents

Introduction

DOS is something people forget about, until they are forced to use it. But when you need to use DOS to copy files or create directories, who wants to wade through thick manuals to find out how to do something that should take only a few minutes?

With your busy schedule, what you want is a simple, straightforward guide that teaches what you need to know, when you need to know it.

A few things are certain:

- You need a way to move around the MS-DOS 6 Shell without much fuss.

- You need to learn the tasks necessary to accomplish your particular goals.

- You need a clear-cut, plain-English guide to learn about the basic features of MS-DOS.

You need the *10 Minute Guide to MS-DOS 6.*

What Is the 10 Minute Guide?

The *10 Minute Guide* series is designed to help you learn new programs fast. Through a series of lessons which take less than 10 minutes each, you can quickly master the basic skills needed to copy, delete and undelete files, to create and remove directories, and to perform regular backups using MS-DOS 6.

Best of all, you do not have to spend any time figuring out what to learn. All the most important tasks are covered in this *10 Minute Guide*. There's no need for long classes or thick manuals. Learn the skills you need in short, easy-to-follow lessons.

Conventions Used in This Book

Each of the short lessons in this book include step-by-step instructions for performing specific tasks. The following icons will help you identify particular types of information:

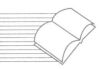

Plain English icons help you learn the terms you'll need to know in order to understand MS-DOS 6.

Panic Button icons help you avoid making mistakes.

Timesaver Tip icons offer ways to save time when using MS-DOS 6.

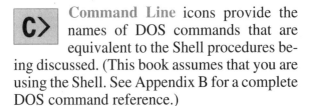

Command Line icons provide the names of DOS commands that are equivalent to the Shell procedures being discussed. (This book assumes that you are using the Shell. See Appendix B for a complete DOS command reference.)

In addition to these icons, look for the following conventions:

`What you type`	Information you type appears in bold, color computer type.
Items you select	Keys you must press or items you must select appear in color.
`On-screen text`	Messages that are displayed on-screen appear in computer type.
Shortcut keys	Shortcut keys for selecting menu items and commands appear in color in this book. The boldface letter corresponds to the bold letter you see on-screen.
Key combinations	In many cases, you must press a two-key combination in order to enter a command (for example, "Press Alt+F"). In such cases, hold down the first key and press the second key, then release both.

Using This Book

On the front inside cover of this book, you will find easy instructions for installing MS-DOS 6 on your system. The back inside cover features a guide to the keyboard shortcuts to use with the MS-DOS 6 Shell.

This book contains over 20 lessons, each covering a specific task for using MS-DOS 6. You should complete each of the lessons, in order, until you feel comfortable using MS-DOS. After Lesson 7, you may want to skip around and complete only those lessons you need for your work.

Because it's easier, this book assumes you are using the DOS Shell. Each lesson also provides equivalent DOS commands, however, for command-line users. Also, Appendix A contains a complete DOS command reference.

For Further Reference . . .

If you decide, after completing this book, that you want a more detailed guide to using MS-DOS 6, I suggest the following books from Alpha Books:

The First Book of MS-DOS 6 by Joe Kraynak

One Minute Reference: MS-DOS 6
by Faithe Wempen

Acknowledgments

I would like to thank all of the wonderful people at Alpha Books, who care about the beginner in all of us.

Trademarks

All terms mentioned in this book that are known to be trademarks or service marks are listed here. In addition, terms suspected of being trademarks or service marks have been appropriately capitalized. Alpha Books cannot attest to the accuracy of this information. Use of a term in this book should not be regarded as affecting the validity of any trademark or service mark.

Lessons

Lesson 1
A First Look at DOS

In this lesson, you will learn how to start your PC. You will also learn more about DOS and what it does.

Starting Your PC

Before you can start learning about DOS, you'll need to start your PC so you'll have a way to practice what you learn. The process of starting a computer is called *booting*. When your PC boots, the disk operating system (DOS) is loaded (copied) into memory. *Memory* is the working area of your PC, where the computer temporarily stores information it needs. You can load DOS in one of two ways:

- **From the hard disk.** This is the most common way to load DOS. To boot a PC in this manner, simply turn on the PC, and DOS is copied from the hard disk into memory.

- **From a diskette.** If your PC does not have a hard disk, you will need to place a special disk (called a *system disk*) in drive A. To boot a PC in this manner, insert the MS-DOS 6 Startup/Support Diskette into drive A, turn the PC on, and DOS is copied from the diskette into memory.

1

Protect Your Investment To protect your original installation diskettes from accidental damage (especially if you use them to start your computer every day), you should make copies of them. If you don't know how to make copies, refer to Lesson 14 for more information.

Booting The process of starting your PC and loading the operating system (DOS) into memory.

Memory The working area of your computer, where the computer stores files temporarily as it works on them.

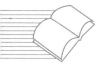

Hard Disk Located inside your PC, the hard disk stores your permanent information, such as programs, documents, and DOS. The hard disk is usually referred to as *drive C*.

Entering the Date and Time

Once your PC is started, it may ask you to verify the current date and time. (If your PC has an internal clock, as most do, you may not see these prompts.) Make sure your system uses the correct date and time, because that is how DOS keeps track of changes. If you see the prompt

```
Current date is 01-01-80
Enter new date:
```

enter the current date (after the colon) in one of three formats. For example:

```
02-20-93

02/20/93

02.20.93
```

If you see the prompt

```
Current time is 00:00:01
Enter new time:
```

enter the current time (after the colon). Use military time (a 24-hour clock). For example, to enter 2:12 p.m., type `14:12` and press Enter. You can also enter the seconds, as in `14:12:33`.

What Is DOS?

DOS is the *disk operating system*, and as such, DOS is responsible for the operation of your computer. For example, a program may tell DOS to read the contents of a file, and DOS takes care of the details. (You'll learn more about files in Lesson 2, but for now, you can visualize placing papers in a file folder.)

Why do you need to know DOS? DOS is the captain of your computer, controlling what it does and when. When you need to do something with the computer, such as copying a file or formatting a diskette, you tell DOS and it gets done. Learning more about DOS puts you in better control of your computer, and allows you to perform your daily computing tasks with greater ease.

Using the DOS Command Line Versus Using the DOS Shell

DOS 6 provides two ways for you to give it instructions: the *DOS command line* and the *DOS Shell*. When you use the DOS command line, you enter a string of characters at the *DOS prompt*. The DOS prompt looks something like C> or C:\>.

To enter a DOS command, you type the command after the DOS prompt. For example, the MEM command tells DOS to report how much available memory it has. You enter the command after the greater-than sign (>), as shown in Figure 1.1.

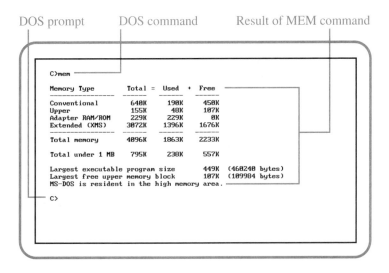

DOS prompt DOS command Result of MEM command

```
C>mem

Memory Type        Total =  Used  +  Free
-------------      ------   ------   ------
Conventional        640K     190K     450K
Upper               155K      48K     107K
Adapter RAM/ROM     229K     229K       0K
Extended (XMS)     3072K    1396K    1676K
-------------      ------   ------   ------
Total memory       4096K    1863K    2233K

Total under 1 MB    795K     238K     557K

Largest executable program size     449K  (460240 bytes)
Largest free upper memory block     107K  (109984 bytes)
MS-DOS is resident in the high memory area.

C>
```

Figure 1.1 Entering commands at the DOS prompt.

After you type the command, press the Enter key; DOS then performs the command. (When you press Enter after typing MEM, a report telling you how much memory your computer has available appears on the monitor.)

If you have at least MS-DOS 4, you can issue commands not only from the command line, but from the DOS Shell. The DOS Shell, shown in Figure 1.2, is much easier for a new user to understand and to use than the command-line prompt.

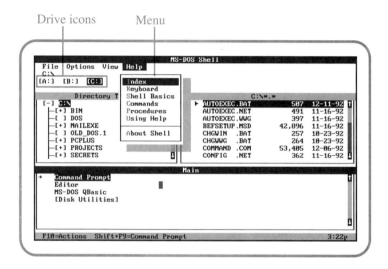

Figure 1.2 Using the DOS Shell to issue commands is easier.

With the DOS Shell, you enter commands by selecting them from menus. A *menu* presents a list of choices for you to select from—with menus, you don't have to memorize command names in order to perform a DOS task. You'll learn more about menus in Lesson 5.

Menu A menu is a list of possible tasks or commands. With a menu, the user doesn't memorize anything, but simply makes a choice from the options presented.

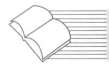

5

Some commands in the DOS Shell are issued by selecting a picture called an *icon*. You'll learn more about the DOS Shell and using icons in Lesson 4.

 Taking It Easy   This book assumes that you are using the DOS Shell, because it is the easiest way to use DOS. The DOS Shell described in this book is the DOS 6 Shell, which is nearly identical to the DOS 5 Shell. (The DOS 4 Shell is substantially different.) If you prefer to enter commands at the DOS prompt, see Appendix A for a command prompt reference.

What Is AUTOEXEC.BAT?

The DOS 6 installation program creates a file called AUTOEXEC.BAT. AUTOEXEC.BAT is a special file that executes commands automatically when you start your computer.

In addition to the commands placed in the AUTOEXEC.BAT by the DOS 6 installation program, you can add your own commands to be executed at startup. For example, you could place a command in the AUTOEXEC.BAT to automatically start the DOS Shell or some other program for you. You'll learn more about the AUTOEXEC.BAT file in future lessons.

What Is CONFIG.SYS?

The CONFIG.SYS file is used to customize DOS. Certain system defaults, such as the number of files that can be opened at one time, must be changed in order for certain programs to function properly on your system.

As it does with the AUTOEXEC.BAT, the DOS 6 installation program places certain commands in the CONFIG.SYS file for you. For example, if you chose to load the Anti-virus program during DOS 6 installation, commands are placed in the CONFIG.SYS to start the Anti-virus program when you boot your computer. You'll learn more about the CONFIG.SYS file in future lessons.

In this lesson, you learned how to start your computer. You also learned about DOS and the role it plays. In the next lesson, you'll learn about disks, directories, and files.

What Are Disks, Directories, and Files?

In this lesson, you will learn some basic computer terms: disks, directories, and files.

What Are Disks?

There are two types of disks that your computer uses: *hard disks* and *floppy disks*. Hard disks are for permanent storage of files and programs. Floppy disks (often called *diskettes*) are for portable (removable) storage.

Your computer's hard disk (usually drive C) is used to store your programs, documents, and DOS. You can copy these files onto diskettes, where they serve as backups in case the hard disk gets damaged in some way.

Diskettes are small plastic squares which are inserted into a slot in the front of your computer. Diskettes come in two sizes: 5 1/4 inches and 3 1/2 inches, as shown in Figure 2.1. Each size diskette comes in *high-density* and *double-density* versions (3 1/2-inch diskettes also come in an *extended-density* version).

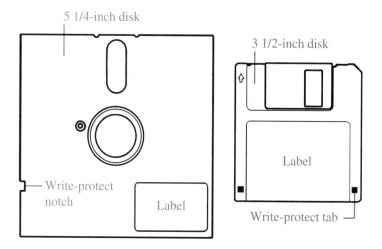

Figure 2.1 Diskettes come in two sizes.

Density The amount of information that a diskette can hold. High-density diskettes hold at least twice as much information as the same size double-density diskettes because the information on high-density diskettes is packed closer together. Extended-density diskettes (which only come in the 3 1/2-inch size) hold twice as much information as 3 1/2-inch high-density diskettes.

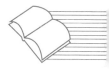

It's Your Density! Purchase diskettes that match the type of diskette drive your computer uses. This means you have to buy not only the right size diskette (5 1/4-inch or 3 1/2-inch), *but also the right density* (high density, double density, or extended density).

   Disk drives are assigned letters. Your computer's first diskette drive is called A, and a second drive is called B.

Your computer's hard disk is called C, and additional hard disks are called D, E, and so on. Disks are represented by their drive letter, followed by a colon, as in C: and A:.

What Are Files?

Hard disks and diskettes are used to store your computer *data* (data is a computer term for information). You save your computer data in files, which are like tiny books. You store different kinds of data in different files. For example, you might store a memo in one file, a picture of a boat in another file, and the fiscal budget in yet another file. Each file has its own name, just like a book, as shown in Figure 2.2.

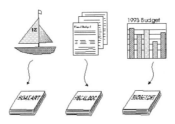

Figure 2.2 Files are like books, with their own names.

File names can have up to eight *characters* (letters or numbers). Most file names also have an *extension*, which helps to identify the contents or purpose of the file. For example, if you named a file BUDGET.DOC, the extension .DOC would identify the file as a document file. Some programs use special extensions to identify their own files. For example, Lotus 1-2-3 uses either .WKS or .WK1 to identify its worksheet files.

What Are Directories?

With so many files, how does your computer keep track of them? To use an analogy, book stores and libraries organize books according to subject. In a similar manner, files on your hard disk are typically organized by subject or purpose. For example, the files for your word processing program are kept in one place, while the files for your spreadsheet program are kept in another.

In book stores and libraries, books are placed on shelves. On disks, files are placed in directories. One special directory is called the *root directory*. Think of the root directory as the lobby of a building; just as rooms branch off from a lobby, other directories branch off from the root. Only general-purpose files (such as the CONFIG.SYS and AUTOEXEC.BAT files) should be placed in the root directory. The root directory is represented by a single backslash (\), so the root directory of drive C is C:\.

Branching out from the root directory, you create other directories, one for each program you use. If you think of these directories as rooms, you could have a room for word processing, a room for spreadsheets, a room for drawing, and so on. These directories (or rooms) connect to the root directory (the lobby), as shown in Figure 2.3.

You can separate the files you create (documents) from the program files by creating subdirectories. To continue our room analogy, you could think of subdirectories as closets within each room. Directories are represented by a backslash, followed by the name of the directory, as in C:\WORD. Subdirectories are separated from their parent by another backslash, as in C:\WORD\DOCS.

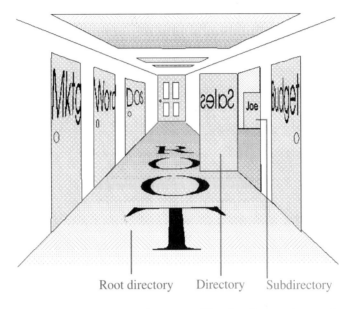

Root directory   Directory   Subdirectory

Figure 2.3 Organize your files in directories and subdirectories.

Keeping Organized The way you organize the files on your hard disk is up to you. Keeping your files organized makes it easier to use them.

In this lesson, you learned what disks, files, and directories are. In the next lesson, you will learn how to start and exit the DOS Shell.

Lesson 3

Starting and Exiting the DOS Shell

In this lesson, you will learn how to start and exit the DOS Shell. You will also learn how to use a mouse.

Starting the DOS Shell

The DOS Shell is a *graphical interface*. A graphical interface uses pictures (called *icons*) to represent things such as drives and directories. The idea is that pictures are easier to understand than a bunch of confusing commands. The Shell lets you perform common DOS commands more easily than you could with the DOS prompt. You can configure the DOS Shell so that it runs automatically when you boot your PC. If the DOS Shell doesn't run at startup, you can run the DOS Shell manually by typing DOSSHELL and pressing Enter. You will then see a screen similar to Figure 3.1.

The DOS Shell has many parts:

Menu bar   Displays a list of pull-down menus.

Drive listing   Displays a list of drives.

Directory Tree   Displays a list of directories for the active drive.

File List   Displays a list of files in the active directory.

Program List   Displays a list of programs you can run, and program groups (collections of related programs).

Status bar   Displays a list of keys you can press to activate the menu bar or the DOS prompt.

Directory Tree   Menu bar   Drive listing

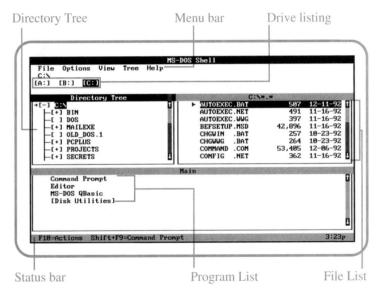

Status bar   Program List   File List

Figure 3.1   The DOS Shell opening screen.

Basic Mouse Techniques

When you use the DOS Shell, I recommend performing most of the basic tasks with a mouse. A *mouse* is a device attached to your computer which controls a pointer on your screen. To move the pointer to the left, move the mouse to the left. To move the pointer to the right, move the mouse to the right, and so on. To initiate most actions with the mouse, you either click or double-click; always use the left mouse button *unless told specifically to use the right.*

Click   To click with the mouse, press the mouse button once.

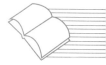

Double-click   To double-click with the mouse, press the mouse button twice in rapid succession.

Some actions require that you *drag* the mouse.

Drag   To drag the mouse, first move the mouse to the starting position. Now click and hold the mouse button. Drag the mouse to the ending position and then release the mouse button.

To select a menu command with the mouse, click once on the menu name, and the menu freezes in the *drop-down*, or open, position. You can then move the mouse down the open menu list to the selection you want.

Selecting a Menu Command in One Step   Click and hold the mouse button as you drag it down the menu. Release the mouse button when the selection you want is highlighted.

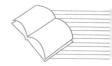

Exiting the DOS Shell

To exit the DOS Shell and return to the DOS prompt (c>), follow these steps:

1. Click on File in the menu bar to open the File menu, as shown in Figure 3.2. If you don't own a mouse, press F10 to activate the menu bar, and press F.

2. Click on Exit, or press X.

File menu

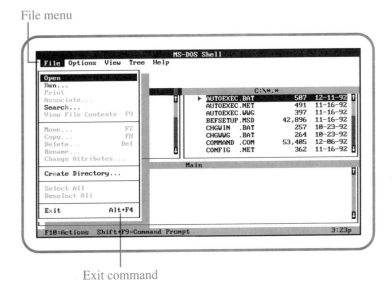

Exit command

Figure 3.2 Click on the File menu to open it.

The DOS Shell will then remove itself from memory and return you to the DOS prompt.

Fast Exit   To exit the DOS Shell quickly, press F3.

Exiting the DOS Shell Temporarily

You may want to leave the Shell temporarily to enter commands directly at the DOS command line. When you follow this procedure, the Shell is kept in memory, waiting until you come back to it.

To exit the DOS Shell temporarily:

1. Press Shift+F9 or click on Command Prompt in the Program List. The DOS prompt will display, as shown in Figure 3.3.

Enter any DOS command you want.   DOS message

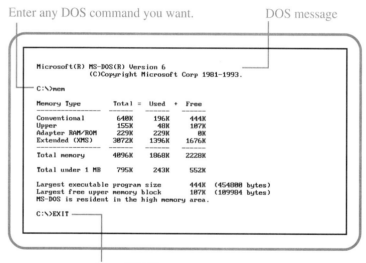

```
Microsoft(R) MS-DOS(R) Version 6
        (C)Copyright Microsoft Corp 1981-1993.

C:\>mem

Memory Type        Total  =  Used  +  Free
--------------     ------    ------    ------
Conventional        640K      196K      444K
Upper               155K       48K      107K
Adapter RAM/ROM     229K      229K        0K
Extended (XMS)     3072K     1396K     1676K
                   ------    ------    ------
Total memory       4096K     1868K     2228K

Total under 1 MB    795K      243K      552K

Largest executable program size      444K  (454800 bytes)
Largest free upper memory block      107K  (109984 bytes)
MS-DOS is resident in the high memory area.

C:\>EXIT
```

Type EXIT to return to Shell.

Figure 3.3   You can exit the Shell temporarily by pressing Shift+F9.

2. Enter any valid DOS command.

3. When you are ready to return to the DOS Shell, type EXIT at the prompt and press Enter.

Too Many Exits? To leave the DOS Shell permanently, press F3. To leave the DOS Shell temporarily, press Shift+F9. To return to the DOS Shell after leaving it temporarily, type EXIT.

In this lesson, you learned how to start and exit the DOS Shell. You also learned about the main parts of the DOS Shell window, and how to use a mouse. In the next lesson, you will learn how to move around the Shell window, and how to get help.

Lesson 4

Navigating the DOS Shell

In this lesson, you will learn how to move around the
DOS Shell, and how to access the Help system.

Changing the Display Mode

When you start the DOS Shell, it starts in Text mode. *Text
mode* can be used on all types of computer monitors. Text
mode uses boxes and lines to represent the Shell icons, such
as the disk drive and directory icons. If your PC has a
monitor that supports graphics, you can change the DOS
Shell display to *Graphics mode*, as shown in Figure 4.1.
(For a comparison, look back at Figure 3.1, which depicts
the Shell in Text mode.)

To change the DOS Shell to Graphics mode, follow
these steps:

1. Open the Options menu by clicking on it. If you do not
   have a mouse, press F10 to activate the menu bar, then
   press O. (You'll learn quicker ways to issue menu
   commands in the next lesson.)

2. Select the Display... command by clicking on it. If you
   are using the keyboard, use the arrow keys to highlight

the Display... command and press Enter. A dialog box, shown in Figure 4.2, will appear (you'll learn more about dialog boxes in the next lesson).

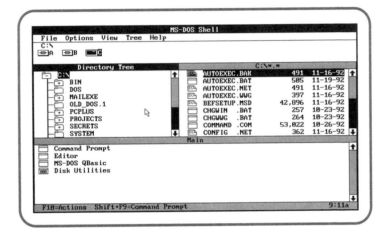

Figure 4.1 The DOS Shell in Graphics mode.

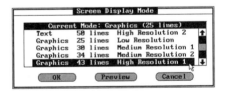

Figure 4.2 The Display dialog box.

3. Click on the desired graphics resolution, or use the arrow keys to highlight a Graphics selection, and press Enter. Your screen will change to Graphics mode, as shown in Figure 4.1.

Reading the Fine Print   The higher the resolution, the greater the number of lines which will display, but the letters appear tinier. So, if you select a high resolution (such as Graphics 43 Lines), more files and directories will appear on-screen, but the letters will be smaller and harder to read. Make sure you feel comfortable with the resolution you select.

Moving Around the Shell Window

The DOS Shell window is made up of several sections as shown in Figure 4.3:

- Drive listing

- Directory Tree

- File List

- Program List

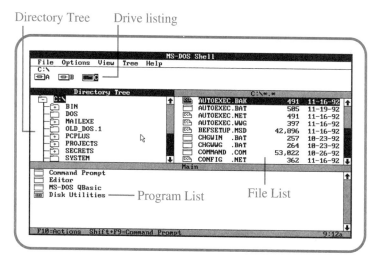

Figure 4.3 The DOS Shell window is divided into sections.

To move from section to section with the mouse, you simply click inside that section. To move from section to section with the keyboard, press the Tab key. To move backward from section to section, press Shift+Tab.

The active section is highlighted, as shown in Figure 4.3.

Changing Drives

Now that you know how to move around the DOS Shell window, you can change the display so it reflects the contents of another drive, such as drive A. This is called *changing drives*. The current drive is highlighted, as shown in Figure 4.3.

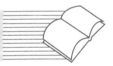 **Changing Drives**   Changing the directory and file displays so they list the contents of a drive other than the current drive.

To select drive A in the Drive listing:

1. Press Tab to activate the Drive listing section.

2. Use the arrow keys to highlight drive A and press Enter.

If you use a mouse, you can simply click on the drive A icon. The Directory Tree and the File List will change to reflect the contents of drive A. To change drives in one step, press Ctrl+*drive*. For example, to change to drive A, press Ctrl+A.

 Command Line Users   To change drives at the DOS command line, enter the drive letter followed by a colon, as in A: or C:.

Getting Help

Getting help within the DOS Shell is easy. Anytime you need help, simply press F1. For example, if the Program List is active, and the selection Command Prompt is highlighted, when you press F1, you will see a screen like the one shown in Figure 4.4.

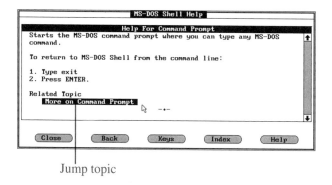

Jump topic

Figure 4.4   It's easy to get help in the DOS Shell.

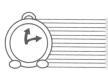

Taking the Easy Way Out   To exit Help, press Esc.

The DOS Shell Help system is *context-sensitive*. This means that when you press F1, you will be taken to a specific part of the Help system which contains information on the task you were trying to complete.

Tell Me More   Some Help topics contain more information than can be displayed on a single screen. To see more, press the Page Down key.

Some Help windows provide a quick means of getting additional information, called *jump topics*. For example, if you wanted more information on the DOS command prompt, you would select the related jump topic, More on Command Prompt. To select a jump topic:

• Press Tab until the topic is highlighted, and press Enter.

OR

• Double-click on the desired topic.

Command Line Users   To get Help with a DOS command, type that command, followed by /?. For example, to get Help for the MEM command, type MEM /? or HELP MEM.

In this lesson, you learned how to change the Shell display mode, move around the Shell window, and access Help. In the next lesson, you will learn how to use menus and dialog boxes to issue commands.

Lesson 5

Using Menus and Dialog Boxes

In this lesson, you will learn how to use the DOS Shell's menus and dialog boxes.

Menu Basics

At the top of the DOS Shell window shown in Figure 5.1, there is a menu bar. The menu bar lists the main DOS Shell menus: File, Options, View, Tree, and Help. Under each of these menus, there are additional selections, available on *pull-down menus.*

Pull-down Menu   Contains the selections for a main menu command. This type of menu, when activated, is pulled down below the main menu bar, the way a window shade can be pulled down from the top of a window frame.

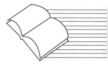

Menus make use of optional conventions:

Grayed text   Commands that are currently unavailable will be grayed to prevent you from selecting them.

Shortcut keys   A single letter of a menu command, such as x in Exit, that can be used to activate the

25

command with the keyboard. Shortcut keys appear as underlined letters on the main menu. In this book, shortcut keys appear as bold letters, as in **F**ile.

Accelerator keys   Like shortcut keys, these can be used to activate the command with the keyboard. Usually a function key (or a key combination, such as Alt+F4), these are displayed next to the menu command.

Ellipsis   An ellipsis consists of three periods after a menu command, such as the **F**ile Sear**c**h... command. An ellipsis indicates that after you choose this command, a dialog box appears, requiring you to provide more specific information before the command is executed.

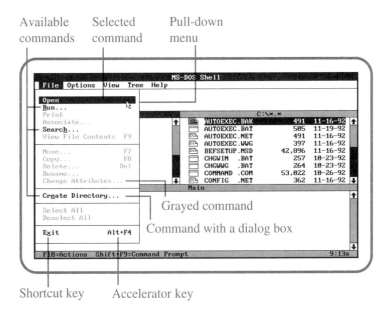

Figure 5.1   DOS Shell's menu system.

Selecting Menu Commands

It's easy to select menu commands using either the mouse or the keyboard. To activate a pull-down menu with the mouse, click once on the menu name.

To activate a pull-down menu with the keyboard:

- Press Alt plus the shortcut key. For example, to activate the File pull-down menu, press Alt+F.

- Alternatively, you can press F10 and then use the arrow keys to activate the appropriate pull-down menu.

Once a menu is visible, you can select a command from it by once again using either the mouse or the keyboard. To select a command from a pull-down menu with the mouse, click once on the pull-down menu command.

To select a command from a pull-down menu with the keyboard:

- Use the arrow keys to highlight the command, and then press Enter.

OR

- Press the shortcut key letter for the command. For example, with the File menu open, you can select the Search... command by pressing the letter H.

Using Dialog Boxes

When you select a menu command that requires additional information, a dialog box appears. Commands that display a dialog box appear on menus with an ellipsis following their names. A typical dialog box is shown in Figure 5.2.

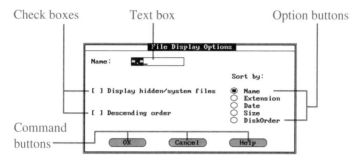

Figure 5.2 A typical dialog box.

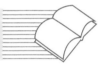 **Dialog Box** A special window which appears when the DOS Shell requires additional information before executing a command.

There are a few optional components of dialog boxes:

List box Presents a list of items to choose from, such as a list of files.

Text box Allows the user to type or edit information, such as the name of a file.

Drop-down list box Displays under the main list item, like a windowshade. Drop-down list boxes are like normal list boxes, except that the list does not display until activated.

Check box Indicates options that can be turned on or off, such as Read Only.

Option button   Selects mutually exclusive options, such as sorting files by name or extension.

Command button   Performs some specific command, such as OK or Cancel.

Making Choices in a Dialog Box

In some dialog boxes, you will be presented with many different components, such as list boxes and option buttons, where you need to make several choices. You can use either the mouse or the keyboard when making these choices in a dialog box.

To move between the components in a dialog box:

* With the mouse, you can move freely between components in a dialog box by clicking on any item.

* With the keyboard, press Tab or Shift+Tab to move forward or backward.

To select an item:

* With the mouse, simply click on an item to select it.

* With the keyboard, use the arrow keys. In a list box, you may also use the Home, End, Page Up, and Page Down keys.

To toggle an option button or check box on or off:

* With the mouse, click on the option button or check box to toggle it on or off.

- With the keyboard, select the option button or check box, and then use the Spacebar to toggle it on or off.

There are some standard command buttons you can select in dialog boxes:

OK　Select this button to close the dialog box and execute the choices you made.

Cancel　Select this button to cancel the choices you have made in the dialog box, and return to the DOS Shell.

Help　Select this button to obtain help for this dialog box.

In this lesson, you learned how to use menus and dialog boxes. In the next lesson, you will learn how to control the DOS Shell window.

Lesson 6
Controlling the Shell Window

In this lesson, you will learn how to control the file and directory information that appears in the Shell window.

Changing Directories

The Shell window displays the contents of the current drive. If drive C is the current drive, a complete directory listing of drive C is displayed in the Directory Tree window, and the files that are contained in the root directory of drive C are displayed in the File List, as shown in Figure 6.1. (For information on how to change the current drive, see Lesson 4.)

If you wish to see the contents of another directory, such as \DOS, you must change the current directory in the Directory Tree. To change the directory:

1. Activate the Directory Tree by clicking on it or by pressing Tab.

2. Change directories by clicking on a new directory or using the arrow keys to highlight it. The File List will change to display the contents of the new directory.

Active directory   Expanded directory

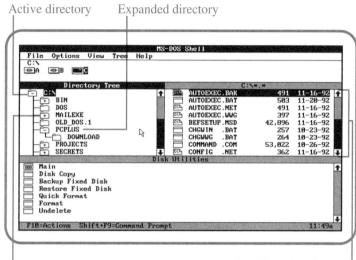

Collapsed directory   Files in active directory

Figure 6.1   The DOS Shell window reflects the contents of the current drive.

 Getting to the Root of It   To move quickly to the root directory, press the backslash key (\ ).

 **Command Line Users**   The equivalent DOS command for changing directories is **CHDIR** or just **CD**.

Changing the Directory Display

Some directories contain subdirectories. For example, you might have a subdirectory under your \WORD directory for your document files, as in \WORD\DOCS. A minus sign indicates directories that contain subdirectories currently displayed (as shown in Figure 6.1). A plus sign indicates directories which are not currently displaying their subdirectories.

You can display or hide subdirectories by expanding or collapsing a branch of the Directory Tree.

Pick a Key, Any Key   For any of the tasks in this section, rather than clicking, you can press the plus (+), minus (–), and asterisk (*) keys—either on the numeric keypad or on the typewriter keys. If you use the typewriter keys, remember to press the Shift key to access + and *.

Expanding a Directory Branch

To expand a directory branch:

1. Select the directory to expand.

2. Click on the + (in front of the directory name) or press plus (+).

Expanding into Other Neighborhoods   When you expand a directory branch, it expands one level. If there are sub-subdirectories, they won't be displayed. Press the asterisk (*) to expand a directory through all of its levels.

Fast Expansion   To expand all branches of the Directory Tree, press Ctrl+asterisk (*).

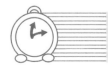

Collapsing a Directory Branch

To collapse a directory branch:

1. Select the branch of the directory you want to collapse.

2. Click on the minus sign (–) in front of the directory name, or press minus (–).

Quick Collapse If you have expanded the entire Directory Tree, and wish to display only the directories off the root: press backslash (\) to move to the root directory, press minus (–) to collapse all directories, then press plus (+) to expand one level.

Changing the Way Files Are Displayed

You can change the way files are displayed in the File List with the **O**ptions **F**ile Display Options command. Select from among these options:

- **Name**   Use this option to select which files are displayed. See the next section, "Using Wildcards to Specify Files," for more information.

- **Display hidden/system files**   Some files (especially those which make up the core of the operating system) are hidden to prevent accidental damage. Use this option to display these files.

- **Sort by**   Use this option to change the way files are sorted in the File List. You can sort files by name, extension, date of last change, size, and placement on the disk.

- **Descending order**   Use this option to sort files in reverse order. For example, if Name sort is being used, this option will cause the files to sort from Z to A.

To change the way file information is displayed:

1. Open the Options menu.

2. Select the File Display Options command. The File Display Options dialog box will appear, as shown in Figure 6.2.

Figure 6.2   The File Display Options dialog box.

3. Select the desired options, and click on OK or press Enter.

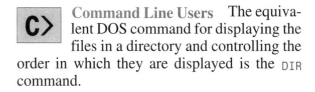   **Command Line Users**   The equivalent DOS command for displaying the files in a directory and controlling the order in which they are displayed is the DIR command.

Using Wildcards to Specify Files

To display a group of files based on their names, use *wildcards*. DOS provides two wildcards for this purpose:

- The **asterisk (*)** stands for consecutive characters in a filename.

  For example, to select all the files that end in .DOC (such as CHAMPION.DOC and FUNDRASR.DOC), type *.DOC.

  To select all the files that begin with BUDGET (such as BUDGET92.WKS, BUDGET93.WKS, and BUDGET93.CHT), type BUDGET*.*.

  To select all the files in a directory, use *.*.

- The **question mark (?)** stands for a single character in a filename.

  For example, to select the files CHAP1.DOC through CHAP9.DOC (but not CHAP10.DOC), type CHAP?.DOC.

 Command Line Users If you use the DOS command line to issue commands, you'll be using wildcards more often than in the DOS Shell. On the command line, there is no method for selecting more than one file other than with wildcards (in the DOS Shell, you select files by highlighting them— you'll learn more about this in Lesson 7).

Displaying Dual File Lists

Some DOS functions, such as copying files or moving them from one directory to another, are easier with a dual list display, as shown in Figure 6.3.

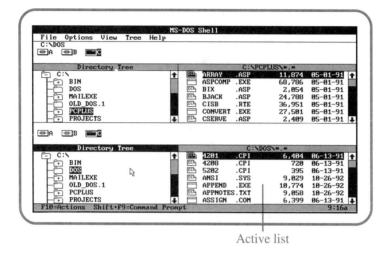

Active list

Figure 6.3 Using dual file lists can make some DOS functions easier.

To display dual file lists:

1. Open the View menu.

2. Select the Dual File Lists command. Two file lists will appear.

   To return to a single file list:

1. Open the View menu.

2. Select either Single File List or Program/File Lists (to display both a single file list and the Program List).

Repainting or Refreshing the File List

Some DOS functions, such as deleting files, may cause the File List to become out-of-date. To force the DOS Shell to reread the disk and update the list of files:

1. Open the View menu.

2. Select the Refresh command.

Equally Refreshing To refresh the File List quickly, press F5.

Occasionally, you may want to redraw the display (for example, if part of a dialog box remains on the screen after you've closed it). To repaint (redraw) the display:

1. Open the View menu.

2. Select the Repaint Screen command.

In this lesson, you learned how to control the information that is displayed in the Directory Tree and File List windows. In the next lesson, you will learn how to select files.

Lesson 7
Selecting Files

In this lesson, you will learn how to select files in the Shell so you can perform various DOS functions with them.

Selecting a Group of Files

Before you can perform any DOS function which involves files, such as copying, deleting, or moving, you must first select the file you want to work on. You can select more than one file if you want to perform some DOS functions on a group of files. When a file is selected, it is highlighted in the File List, as shown in Figure 7.1.

To select a single file, simply click on it with the mouse, or use the arrow keys to highlight it. To select several files, use one of the techniques described in the following sections.

Want It All?   To select all the files in the current directory quickly, press Ctrl+slash (/).

Selected files

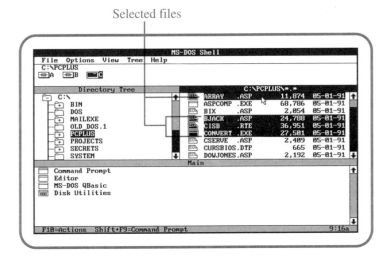

Figure 7.1 Selected files are highlighted in the File List.

Selecting Contiguous Files

Files that are together in a list are *contiguous*, as shown in Figure 7.2.

Contiguous Files Files that are listed next to each other in the File List.

To select contiguous files with the mouse:

1. Click on the first file you want to select.

2. Press and hold the Shift key.

3. Click on the last file you want to select.

Contiguous files

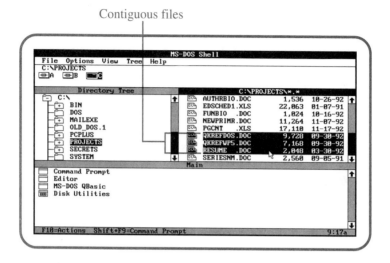

Figure 7.2   You can select files that are contiguous in a list.

To select contiguous files with the keyboard:

1. If necessary, press Tab to move to the File List.

2. Use the arrow keys to move to the first file you want to select.

3. Press and hold the Shift key.

4. Use the arrow keys to move down the list until all the files you want are selected. The files are highlighted.

Selecting Noncontiguous Files

Files that are not together in the File List are *noncontiguous*, as shown in Figure 7.3.

41

Noncontiguous files

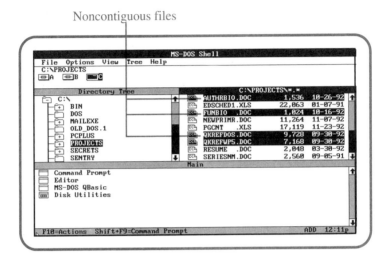

Figure 7.3 You can select files that are noncontiguous in a list.

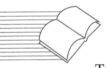

Noncontiguous Files Files that are located in different sections of the File List.

To select noncontiguous files with the mouse:

1. Click on the first file you want to select.

2. Press and hold the Ctrl key.

3. Click on the additional files you want to select. The noncontiguous files are now highlighted. To deselect a file, hold down Ctrl, and click on it again.

To select noncontiguous files with the keyboard:

1. If necessary, press Tab to move to the File List.

2. Use the arrow keys to move to the first file you want to select.

3. Press Shift+F8. The word Add appears in the status bar, as shown in Figure 7.3.

4. Use the arrow keys to move down the list to an additional file you want to select.

5. Press the Spacebar to select the additional file.

6. Repeat steps 4 and 5 until all the files are highlighted. To deselect a file, move to that file and press the Spacebar again.

It Doesn't Add Up To exit Add mode, press Shift+F8 again.

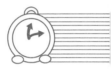

Selecting Files Across Directories

You can select files in several directories by following these steps:

1. Open the Options menu.

2. Choose the Select Across Directories command.

3. Change from directory to directory, selecting the files you want. Perform any DOS function with the selected group of files. To turn off this option (so you select only the files in a single directory), repeat steps 1 and 2.

In this lesson, you learned how to select files. In the next lesson, you will learn how to copy files.

Lesson 8

Copying and Moving Files

In this lesson, you will learn how to copy and move files.

A Word Before You Copy or Move Files

Before you begin to copy or move files, you may want to review the steps for selecting files, covered in Lesson 7. Also, if you notice that files from other directories are being selected (and you don't want them to be), turn off the Select Across Directories command on the Options menu.

 Command Line Users The equivalent DOS command for copying files is COPY. There is no equivalent command for moving files; you must copy them to a new directory then use the DEL command to delete the originals.

Copying Files with the Mouse

When you copy files, the original file is left alone, and a copy is placed in the directory you indicate.

Seeing Double Copying files from directory to directory with the mouse is easier with a dual list display. For more information, see Lesson 6.

Copying files with the mouse is easy:

1. Select the files to copy.

2. Press and hold the Ctrl key.

3. Drag the files to the directory in the Directory Tree (not the File List) where you want them copied. The universal No symbol (a circle with a diagonal slash through it) will appear, but as you move the icon to a valid directory on the screen, it will change, as shown in Figure 8.1.

Files icon

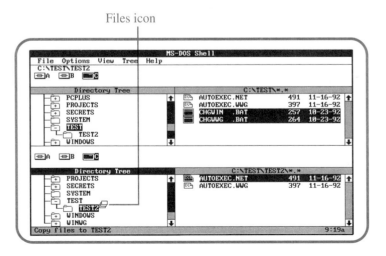

Figure 8.1 Copying files with the mouse.

4. Release the mouse button, and a confirmation box will appear, asking if you really want to copy the files.

5. Click on Yes.

You Look Familiar ... If you attempt to copy a file into a directory where it already exists, DOS will ask you if you want to replace (overwrite) the original file with the one you are copying. Answer Yes to copy the file.

Fast Copies If you are copying files from one drive to another (for example, from drive A to drive C), you do not need to hold down the Ctrl key. That's because the default function, *when you're dragging files from one drive to another*, is the Copy command.

Copying Files with the Keyboard

Copying files with the keyboard is not as easy as with a mouse:

1. Select the files to copy.

2. Open the File menu.

3. Select the Copy command. The Copy File dialog box will appear, as shown in Figure 8.2.

4. The selected files will appear in the From box. Type the destination directory in the To box.

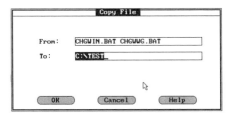

Figure 8.2 The Copy File dialog box.

For example, to copy files to a directory called WORK on drive C, type `C:\WORK`.

To copy files to a subdirectory called MAYCO which is under a directory called PROJECTS on drive C, type `C:\PROJECTS\MAYCO`.

To copy files to the default directory on another drive, type the drive letter, as in `A:`.

To copy files to some directory other than the default on another drive, type the drive letter and the directory, as in `D:\JANE`.

5. Press Enter, and the files are copied.

Quick Copy To copy files quickly, select them and press F8.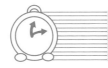

Moving Files with the Mouse

When you move files, the original is deleted and a copy is placed in the selected directory. Moving files with the mouse is similar to copying them:

1. Select the files to move.

2. Press and hold the Alt key.

3. Drag the files to the directory in the Directory Tree (not the File List) where you want them moved. The universal No symbol will appear, but as you move the icon to a valid directory on the screen, it will change to a files icon.

4. Release the mouse button, and a confirmation box will appear, asking you if you really want to move the files.

5. Click on Yes.

 **Fast Moves**   If you are moving files from one directory to another *on the same drive* (for example, from C:\SALES to C:\MARKETNG), you do not need to hold down the Alt key. That's because the default function, *when you're dragging files from one directory to another on the same drive*, is the **M**ove command.

Moving Files with the Keyboard

Moving files with the keyboard is similar to copying files:

1. Select the files to copy.

2. Open the File menu.

3. Select the Move command. The Move File dialog box will appear, as shown in Figure 8.3.

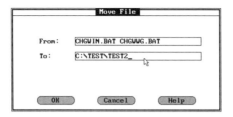

Figure 8.3   The Move File dialog box.

4. The selected files will appear in the From box. Type the destination directory in the To box.

   For example, to move files to a directory called WORK on drive C, type `C:\WORK`.

   To move files to a subdirectory called MAYCO which is under a directory called PROJECTS on drive C, type `C:\PROJECTS\MAYCO`.

   To move files to the default directory on another drive, type the drive letter, as in `A:`.

   To move files to some directory other than the default on another drive, type the drive letter and the directory, as in `D:\JANE`.

5. Press Enter, and the files are moved.

Quick Moves   To move files quickly, select them and press F7.

   In this lesson, you learned how to copy and move files. In the next lesson, you'll learn how to rename files and directories.

Renaming Files and Directories

In this lesson, you will learn how to rename files and directories.

Valid File and Directory Names

The names of files must follow certain conventions:

- File names may contain up to eight characters plus an optional three character extension.

- A valid character is:

  Any letter, from A to Z.

  Any single digit number, from 0 to 9.

  One of these special characters: $ # & @ ! % ( ) - { } '
  _ ` ^ ~

- Uppercase is the same as lowercase. For example, the filename WORK.DOC is the same as work.doc.

- An invalid character is:

  A space

  Any of these special characters: " . / \ [ ] : * < > | + ; , ?

- Use a period only to separate the filename from the extension, as in BUDGET.DOC. You cannot include a period as part of the filename.

Directory names follow the exact same conventions as filenames, *although most users do not use an extension when naming a directory* (you can, if you want). For example, you could name a directory SALES.93 instead of just SALES, but that would be confusing (the directory could easily be mistaken for a file.)

Renaming a File or Directory

To rename a file or directory, follow these steps:

1. Select the file or directory to rename.

2. Open the File menu.

3. Select the Rename command. The Rename File or Rename Directory dialog box will appear, as shown in Figure 9.1.

4. Enter the new name for the file or directory in the New name... text box. Type the complete name, including the extension.

   For example, to change the name of a file to BUDGET93.WKS, type the full name BUDGET93.WKS.

5. Press Enter or click on OK, and the file or directory is renamed.

Figure 9.1 The Rename File dialog box is similar to the Rename Directory dialog box.

Everyone's Changing Their Names You can rename more than one file or directory at a time by selecting them *before* using the File Rename command. A different dialog box will appear for each file or directory you selected.

Command Line Users The equivalent DOS command for renaming files is REN. To rename a directory, use the MOVE command.

In this lesson, you learned how to rename files and directories. In the next lesson, you will learn how to delete files and get them back.

Lesson 10

Deleting Files and Getting Them Back

In this lesson, you will learn how to delete files and restore files that have been deleted accidentally.

Deleting Files

You will find yourself deleting files for many reasons: the files are outdated and you no longer use them, or you need to make room on your hard drive.

Making Room If you are trying to relieve a congested hard drive, use the techniques described in Lesson 17 to back up selected files. Then follow the instructions in this lesson to delete the original files. If you ever need the files again, you can restore them from your backup disks.

Deleting Directories If you want to delete an entire directory, refer to the instructions in Lesson 12.

To delete files:

1. Select the files to delete.

2. Press the Del key. If you've selected more than one file, the Delete File dialog box will appear as shown in Figure 10.1.

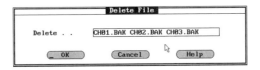

Figure 10.1 When you delete more than one file, a list of files is displayed.

3. Select OK.

4. The Delete Files Confirmation dialog box is displayed for each file selected.

5. Select Yes to confirm the deletion of each file. To bypass a file (not delete it), select No.

Cancel Your Order To cancel the delete files operation, press Esc at any time during the delete process.

You can use the Confirmation command to prevent the Delete Files Confirmation dialog box from appearing:

1. Open the Options menu.

2. Select the Confirmation... command. The Confirmation dialog box will appear.

3. Turn off the Confirm on Delete option.

4. Select OK.

 Command Line Users The equivalent DOS command for deleting files is DEL.

Getting Files Back

If you accidentally delete a file, don't panic. There's a good chance you can get the file back because DOS doesn't actually delete files. Instead of erasing the place on the disk where a file resides, DOS simply erases its *record* of the file—the file's name and location. Because DOS has no record of the file, the deleted file is essentially gone.

So how can you get it back? When DOS erases the file's name from its records, it merely changes the first letter of its name to a question mark, as in ?UDGET.DOC. DOS knows not to pay attention to any file that begins with a question mark, so the space that the file occupies becomes available. If another file needs the disk space, it is written over the deleted file, replacing the old data—so you must act quickly to retrieve deleted files to have any hope of success.

Back to the Future If you delete a file accidentally, *don't do anything!* Follow the steps in this lesson to retrieve the file. If you copy files onto the disk, you may lose your chance to retrieve your lost file—because your copied file may have overwritten the deleted file. Exiting the DOS Shell is also a bad idea, since some temporary files are created when you exit.

A Glimmer of Hope You can greatly improve your chances of recovering deleted files by using Delete Sentry or Delete Tracker, as explained in the next section.

To retrieve a deleted file:

1. Change to the directory that contained the deleted file.

2. From the Program List in the View menu, select Disk Utilities.

3. Select Undelete. The Undelete dialog box, shown in Figure 10.2, appears.

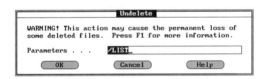

Figure 10.2 The Undelete dialog box.

4. If you know the name of the deleted file, type its name in the Parameters... text box. Otherwise, type *.* to list all the recently deleted files in this directory, and press Enter. A listing of files will appear, as shown in Figure 10.3.

5. Press Y to confirm the undelete procedure. If you do not wish to undelete a particular file, press N. During this process, the list of recently deleted files may be lengthy if you've just done a lot of deleting. To stop the list and return to the Shell, press Esc.

```
Copyright (C) 1987-1993 Central Point Software, Inc.
All rights reserved.

Directory: C:\PROJECTS\TGD
File Specifications: *.*

   Delete Sentry control file contains    3 deleted files.

   Deletion-tracking file contains    0 deleted files.
   Of those,    0 files have all clusters available,
                0 files have some clusters available,
                0 files have no clusters available.

   MS-DOS directory contains    9 deleted files.
   Of those,    6 files may be recovered.

Using the Delete Sentry method.

       CH1     BAK    18432 12-09-92  2:10p  ...A  Deleted:  1-14-93 11:29a
This file can be 100% undeleted. Undelete (Y/N)?y

File successfully undeleted.

       CH2     BAK    16896 12-09-92  2:14p  ...A  Deleted:  1-14-93 11:29a
This file can be 100% undeleted. Undelete (Y/N)?
```

Figure 10.3   Undelete lists recently deleted files.

6. If asked, enter the first letter of the deleted file. (You won't need to do this if you use Delete Sentry, as explained in the next section.) DOS will display a message telling you whether you were successful or not.

7. Repeat steps 5 and 6 until all files have been undeleted.

Do You See What I See?   Your recovered file may not be listed in the File List. Press F5 to refresh the File List window.

 Command Line Users   The equivalent DOS command for recovering deleted files is UNDELETE.

Increasing Your Chances of Recovering Deleted Files

DOS provides two methods for increasing your chances of recovering deleted files:

- **Delete Sentry**   This method provides the best protection, but it may require up to 7% of your hard disk space. When you use this method, a hidden directory called \SENTRY is created. When you delete files, they are copied to this directory before they are deleted by DOS. When you activate Undelete, they are copied back to their original directory. Files are saved in this directory until the \SENTRY directory has grown to 7% of your hard disk space, then old files are deleted to make way for new ones.

- **Delete Tracker**   This method provides better protection than simply relying on fast action on your part. Delete Tracker requires a minimum of disk space, so if your hard disk is almost full, it's a good option. Delete Tracker keeps track of the file's original location on disk in a file called PCTRACKR.DEL, making it easier for DOS to undelete the file.

Using Delete Sentry and Delete Tracker to Protect Files

To install Delete Sentry, place the following command in your AUTOEXEC.BAT file (for information on how to edit your AUTOEXEC.BAT, see Lesson 21):

```
UNDELETE /Sdrive
```

Replace the word *drive* with an actual drive letter, such as C. This drive will hold the /SENTRY directory. For example, to install the /SENTRY directory on your C drive, use this command in your AUTOEXEC.BAT:

```
UNDELETE /SC
```

To install Delete Sentry for a C and a D drive, use this command:

```
UNDELETE /SC /SD
```

If you have limited hard drive space, you might want to use Delete Tracker. Add the following command to your AUTOEXEC.BAT:

```
UNDELETE /Tdrive-numfiles
```

Replace the word *drive* with an actual drive letter, such as C. This drive will hold the file, PCTRACKR.DEL. Replace the word *numfiles* with the maximum number of deleted files you want to keep track of. For example, to install the PCTRACKR.DEL file on your C drive, and track up to 350 deleted files (a good number for a 32MB hard disk), use this command in your AUTOEXEC.BAT:

```
UNDELETE /TC-350
```

To install Delete Tracker for a C and a D drive, use this command to track up to 350 files:

```
UNDELETE /TC-350 /TD-350
```

In this lesson, you learned how to delete files and how to recover them. In the next lesson, you will learn how to search for a file by its name.

Lesson 11

Searching for Files

In this lesson, you will learn how to locate files.

Performing a Search

Searching directories for a file used to be time-consuming. DOS offers you a simple alternative. You can search for a file within a directory, or over the entire hard disk. You can use wildcards (see Lesson 6) to search for files with a particular file name pattern. Follow these steps to perform a search for a file:

1. Open the File menu.

2. Choose Search. The Search File dialog box, shown in Figure 11.1, appears.

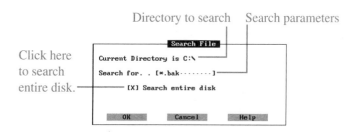

Figure 11.1 The Search File dialog box.

60

3. Type either the name of the file, or a search pattern. (You may use the DOS wild-card characters * and ?.)

4. Select the Search entire disk checkbox if you want the search to continue over the entire disk, not just the current directory.

5. Select OK.

Search and Seizure When a directory is searched, its subdirectories are not searched, unless you are searching the entire disk.

Get Back! To return to the Shell window after searching for files, press Esc.

Command Line Users The equivalent DOS command for searching for files is DIR. When used with the /S switch, the DIR command can search in all subdirectories for a file or file pattern.

Working with the Results of a Search

If a search is successful, a list of files is displayed, as shown in Figure 11.2.

You can perform any file task on the listed files, such as copying, moving, and deleting. To select all the files in the list:

1. Open the File menu.

2. Choose Select All.

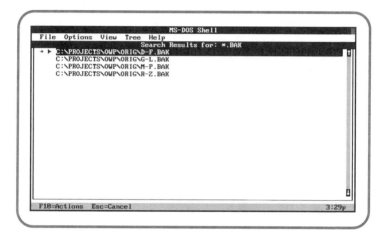

Figure 11.2 A listing of files found in the search is displayed.

See Lesson 7 for information on selecting only certain files.

In this lesson, you learned how to search for files. In the next lesson, you will learn how to manage directories.

Lesson 12
Managing Directories

In this lesson, you will learn how to add and delete directories.

Adding Directories

You can add directories to organize your files and make working with your computer easier. For example, if you use a word processor, you could add a subdirectory (under your word processing directory) called DOCS or WORK to store the documents you create. If you use a spreadsheet program, you could create a similar directory called WKS or XLS. If more than one person uses your computer, create directories where each person can store their files.

To create a directory:

1. If creating a subdirectory, select the parent directory in the Directory Tree. If no directory is selected, the new directory will be a subdirectory of the root.

Directory   Computer files are organized in *directories*. Directories can be thought of as "rooms" on your PC's hard disk; every program you use has its own "room." The files that make up the program are placed in its directory.

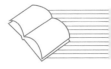

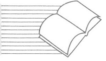

Subdirectory   If a directory is like a room, then a *subdirectory* is like a closet. Subdirectories can be created to further divide a directory's files. For example, you can create a subdirectory called DOCS within the word processing directory for storing your documents. In this way, the word processing directory is the *parent* directory for the subdirectory DOCS.

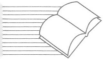

Root directory   The *root directory* is a special directory. You can think of the root directory as a "lobby," and just as rooms branch off of a lobby, directories branch off of the root. Files that are general purpose and not program specific are placed in the root directory, such as AUTOEXEC.BAT and CONFIG.SYS.

2. Open the File menu.

3. Select the Create Directory command. The Create Directory dialog box, shown in Figure 12.1, appears.

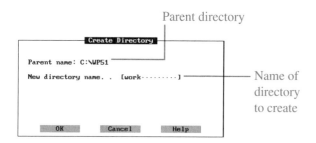

Figure 12.1   The Create Directory dialog box.

4. Type the name of the new directory to create (up to eight characters).

Last Name, Please   You can add up to a three-letter extension to a directory (as in WORK.93), but this is very uncommon and may lead to confusion with file names, which almost always have an extension.

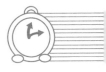

5. Select OK.

 Command Line Users   The equivalent DOS command for creating directories is MD or MKDIR (an abbreviation of "make directory").

Deleting Directories

When a directory is no longer useful, delete it.

Empty Inside   You cannot delete a directory which contains files or subdirectories. You must delete them first. However, there is a DOS command (DELTREE) that you can use instead of the procedure described here. The DELTREE command will delete a directory and all of its subdirectories and files. See Appendix B for details.

1. Select the directory to delete.

2. If necessary, delete all files and subdirectories. For information on deleting files, see Lesson 10.

So Long, Farewell, auf Wiedersehen, Goodnight   If you delete the directory in which files were stored, you may not be able to undelete the files.

3. Press Del.

4. Select Yes.

> **C>** **Command Line Users** The equivalent DOS command for deleting directories is RD. To delete an entire directory tree, including subdirectories and files, use the DELTREE command.

In this lesson, you learned how to add and delete directories. In the next lesson, you will learn how to format diskettes.

Lesson 13
Formatting Diskettes

In this lesson, you will learn how to format diskettes.

A Simple Formatting Procedure

Formatting diskettes prepares them for use and erases all information on the diskette. You need only format a diskette once.

Diskettes must be formatted to the proper density. In Lesson 2, you learned that the *density* of a diskette determines the amount of information it can hold. High-density diskettes hold at least twice as much information as the same size double-density diskettes. If you use diskettes which match the density of your computer's diskette drives, you will not have to worry about formatting them incorrectly. By default, diskettes are formatted to the density of the drive they occupy. (See "When the Diskette Doesn't Match the Drive Type," later in this lesson.)

Make It Quick   If the diskette has already been formatted, and you simply want to erase the files, use the Quick Format command on the Disk Utilities menu.

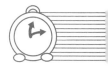

Here's a simple formatting procedure:

1. Place the diskette in the disk drive.

2. Open the Disk Utilities menu in the Program List.

Get Your Programs Here! If the Program List is not displayed, open the View menu and select Program/File Lists.

3. Select the Format command. The Format dialog box appears, shown in Figure 13.1.

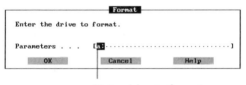

Enter drive to format.

Figure 13.1 The Format dialog box.

4. If necessary, type the drive letter to format, followed by a colon (for example, A:) in the Parameters... text box.

5. Select OK.

6. You will be prompted to insert the diskette. Press Enter, and DOS attempts to save unformatting information, then formats the diskette.

7. After the disk is formatted, you can type an optional volume label, up to 11 characters (including spaces). Press Enter when you are through.

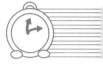

I See You! You can see a disk's volume label while displaying disk information. See Lesson 14 for more information.

8. To format another diskette of the same density, type Y at the Format another (Y/N)? prompt, and press Enter.

9. When you are through, press Enter to return to the DOS Shell.

After a diskette is formatted, DOS displays the amount of space available on the diskette, as shown in Figure 13.2.

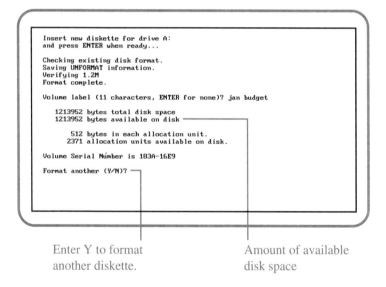

```
Insert new diskette for drive A:
and press ENTER when ready...

Checking existing disk format.
Saving UNFORMAT information.
Verifying 1.2M
Format complete.

Volume label (11 characters, ENTER for none)? jan budget

    1213952 bytes total disk space
    1213952 bytes available on disk

     512 bytes in each allocation unit.
    2371 allocation units available on disk.

Volume Serial Number is 183A-16E9

Format another (Y/N)?
```

Enter Y to format another diskette.

Amount of available disk space

Figure 13.2 DOS displays the amount of space on the formatted diskette.

Command Line Users The equivalent DOS command for formatting diskettes is FORMAT.

Bad Sectors? If bad sectors are found on your diskette, they are marked so that DOS won't use them. You can still use a diskette with bad sectors, but don't use it for irreplaceable information, because such diskettes usually develop additional bad sectors.

Making a Bootable Diskette

A *bootable diskette* can be used to boot your system in the case of an emergency. Prior to DOS 6, a bootable diskette was a staple. If the installation of a new program caused your system to lock up because it made unauthorized changes to your AUTOEXEC.BAT and CONFIG.SYS, you could use the bootable diskette to start your system and make repairs.

Booting The process of starting your PC and loading the operating system (DOS) into memory.

Help Is on the Way! With DOS 6, you can bypass a defective CONFIG.SYS and AUTOEXEC.BAT completely by pressing F5 at startup. Pressing F8 at startup will allow you to select which lines in the CONFIG.SYS and AUTOEXEC.BAT to bypass.

With the new startup feature, a bootable diskette may not be necessary for the same reasons it once was. However, you still need a bootable diskette in case your hard disk becomes inaccessible, or if your system contracts a virus, as explained in Lesson 19. Follow these steps:

1. Complete the usual steps for formatting a diskette, up to step 4.

2. At step 4, enter the drive letter to format, followed by a colon. Then type /s, as in A: /s.

3. Complete the rest of the formatting steps.

The /s parameter tells DOS to copy the system files onto the diskette, making it bootable.

When the Diskette Doesn't Match the Drive Type

If you need to format a diskette which does not match the type of drive your computer uses, you will need to provide additional information:

1. Complete the usual steps for formatting a diskette, up to step 4.

2. At step 4, enter the drive letter to format, followed by a colon. Then type /F: followed by the size of the diskette in bytes, as in A: /F:360.

Just My Size For a double-density 5 1/4-inch diskette, type 360; for a double-density 3 1/2-inch diskette, type 720.

3. Complete the rest of the formatting steps.

Unformatting a Disk

You may be able to unformat a diskette that was formatted accidentally. If you use Delete Sentry (explained in Lesson 10), your chances are even better.

To unformat a diskette:

1. Place the diskette in its drive.

2. Exit the DOS Shell temporarily by pressing Shift+F9.

3. Type UNFORMAT *drive:* where *drive:* is replaced by the letter of the diskette drive, as in UNFORMAT A:.

4. If you want to test the unformat procedure first, you can press the Spacebar and type /TEST, as in UNFORMAT A: / TEST.

5. When prompted, type Y to proceed with the unformat.

6. When the unformat is completed, you can return to the DOS Shell. To return, type EXIT at the prompt.

Can You Keep a Secret? You can protect your sensitive data by formatting a diskette unconditionally. At step 4 in the format procedure, add the /U parameter, as in A: /U. Diskettes formatted in this manner cannot be unformatted.

In this lesson, you learned how to format diskettes. In the next lesson, you will learn how to perform other diskette operations.

Lesson 14

Other Diskette Operations

In this lesson, you will learn how to copy diskettes and how to display disk information.

Copying Diskettes

You should always make a copy of new program diskettes to keep as a backup in case the originals get damaged in some way. You should also make a copy of your original DOS diskettes. In addition, you may want to copy your own work diskettes as backups.

Copy Cat! When copying diskettes, you must use the same size and density as the original.

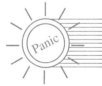

To copy a diskette:

1. Place the original diskette in the drive.

2. Open the Disk Utilities menu in the Program List.

Get Your Programs Here! If the Program List is not displayed, open the View menu and select Program/File Lists.

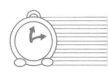

3. Select Disk Copy. The Disk Copy dialog box appears, as shown in Figure 14.1.

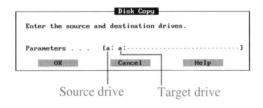

Source drive   Target drive

Figure 14.1 The Disk Copy dialog box.

4. Enter the *source drive* (where the original disk is placed) and *target,* or *destination, drive* (where the target disk is placed). These are often the same drive letters, as in A: A:. Be sure to follow both drive letters with a colon, and separate them with a space.

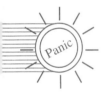

Let's Go for a Drive You must enter two drive letters (such as A: A:) in the Disk Copy dialog box, or you will get the error message Invalid drive specification. Specified drive does not exist or is nonremovable. The first drive letter indicates the source drive, while the second drive letter indicates the target, or destination, drive. You cannot use a drive letter which indicates a hard disk, such as drive C. You can only use diskette drive letters, such as A: and B:.

5. Select OK.

6. Make sure that the source (original) disk is in the drive, then press Enter.

7. When prompted, insert the destination (target) disk in the drive.

8. After the copying procedure is done, you can copy an additional disk by typing Y at the prompt that asks, Copy another diskette?.

9. To return to the DOS Shell, press Enter.

 Command Line Users The equivalent DOS command for copying diskettes is DISKCOPY.

Displaying Disk Information

You can display disk information such as the volume label, available disk space, and number of files with the Show Information command. Information on the selected directory and file(s) will also display.

1. Select the drive or directory for which you want information. If you want information on a group of files (such as the total bytes), select the files you want information on.

2. Open the Options menu.

3. Select Show Information. The Show Information dialog box appears, as shown in Figure 14.2.

4. To return to the DOS Shell, press Esc.

Part of the Group Display information about a group of files by selecting them first, then using the Show Information command.

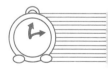

File information　　Total for selected files　　Selected files

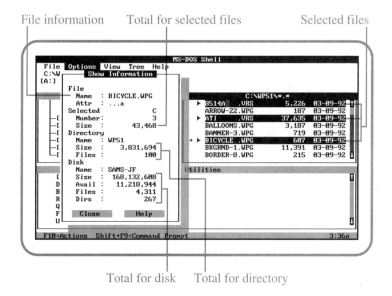

Total for disk　　Total for directory

Figure 14.2 The Show Information dialog box displays available disk space and other important information.

Here's a brief description of the information displayed in the Show Information dialog box:

File information The name of the current file, along with its attributes (if any).

Attributes File attributes include: *hidden* (not displayed in a directory listing), *system* (part of the operating system), *archive* (changed since the last backup), and *read-only* (the file can be read, but not changed).

Selected information The number of files selected, and their total size.

Directory information   The path name of the current directory, the number of files it contains, and their total number of bytes.

Disk information   The volume label of the current disk, its total disk space, the amount of disk space available, the number of files on the disk, and the number of directories.

In this lesson, you learned how to copy diskettes and how to display disk information. In the next lesson, you will learn how to organize the Program List.

Lesson 15

Organizing the Program List

In this lesson, you will learn how to add program groups and program items to the Program List.

Adding New Program Groups

The Program List displays *program groups* (such as Disk Utilities) and *program items* (such as Command Prompt, Editor, and MS-DOS QBasic).

You can add your own programs to the Program List so you can run them from the DOS Shell. Add program groups for related programs, such as utilities, time planning, graphics, games, and so on. Add program items for each application within a program group.

To add a program group:

1. Make the Program List the active window.

Get Your Programs Here! If the Program List is not displayed, open the View menu and select Program/File Lists.

78

2. Open the File menu.

3. Select New. The New Program Object dialog box appears, as shown in Figure 15.1.

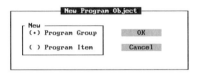

Figure 15.1   Adding a new program group.

4. Select Program Group and OK. The Add Group dialog box appears, shown in Figure 15.2.

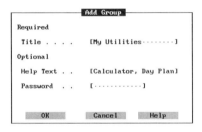

Figure 15.2   The Add Group dialog box.

5. Enter a title (such as My Utilities). The title can be up to 74 characters, including spaces.

6. If you want, you can add Help Text (up to 256 characters) to be displayed when you select the group in the Program List and access Help.

A Little Help from My Friends   Use Help Text to enter a list and a brief description of each program contained in the program group.

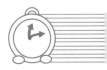

7. If you want, enter a password to prevent unauthorized access to this program group.

8. When you are through, select OK.

Adding New Program Items

A program item represents an individual application, and is used to control how that application is started by the DOS Shell. To add a program item:

1. If the program item should be added to a program group, open that program group first.

 **Open Sesame!** To open a program group and display its program items, either double-click on it, or select it and press Enter.

2. Open the File menu.

3. Select New. The New Program Object dialog box opens.

4. Select Program Item and OK. The Add Program dialog box appears, as shown in Figure 15.3.

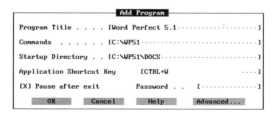

Figure 15.3   Adding a program item.

5. Enter a program title.

6. Enter the command which starts the program, such as WP51.

7. Select any optional features desired:

- If you want to start the program with any special parameters, enter them after the program file name. For example, WordPerfect can be started with a document called JOURNAL.DOC, and instructed to use expanded memory by typing C:\WP51\WP51 JOURNAL.DOC /R on the Commands line.

- Under Startup Directory, enter a directory to be used for any temporary files the program creates.

- Assign a shortcut key to an application for quick access. Use any combination of Shift, Ctrl, and Alt, plus a letter or a number. For example, you can assign the key combination Ctrl+W to your word processing program.

Don't Touch! Don't use any of these key combinations: Ctrl+C, Ctrl+M, Ctrl+I, Ctrl+H, Ctrl+[, Ctrl+5, Shift+Ctrl+M, Shift+Ctrl+I, Shift+Ctrl+H, Shift+Ctrl+[, or Shift+Ctrl+5.

- Add a password under Password to restrict access to this program.

- Select the Pause after exit checkbox to prevent an instant return to the Shell after you exit the program. This option is useful for DOS commands which display information (such as MEM).

81

- If you want to fine-tune how the application starts, select Advanced. The advanced options are discussed in the next section of this lesson.

8. When you are through, select OK.

Changing the Way Programs Run

You can further modify the way programs run with the advanced options. To enter advanced options:

1. From the Add Program dialog box, select Advanced. The Advanced dialog box displays, as shown in Figure 15.4.

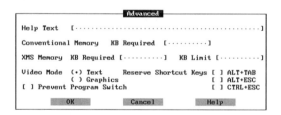

Figure 15.4 Entering advanced options.

2. Select any optional features you want:

- Enter a program description of up to 256 characters in the Help Text box.

- Indicate the program's memory requirements in the Conventional and XMS (expanded memory) boxes.

- Indicate the program's graphics mode (Text or Graphics) under Video Mode.

- If you need to reserve certain shortcut keys for this program's exclusive use, select them under Reserve Shortcut Keys.

- To prevent task-swapping with this program (explained in the next lesson), select the Prevent Program Switch checkbox.

3. When you are through, select OK.

In this lesson, you learned how to add program groups and program items. In the next lesson, you will learn how to run your programs.

Lesson 16

Running Your Programs

In this lesson, you will learn how to run your programs with the DOS Shell.

Selecting a Program to Run

You can select a program to run in several ways:

- Double-click on the program name in the File List.

- Highlight the program name in the File List, and use the Run command on the File menu.

- Double-click on the program item in the Program List.

- Double-click on an associated file.

Running Multiple Programs

DOS includes a *Task Swapper*, which you can use to run more than one program at a time. With this feature, you could use your word processor, jump to your spreadsheet program, then back to your word processor again—without shutting down each program and later restarting it.

When the Task Swapper is enabled, a window (called the Active Task List) appears, as shown in Figure 16.1. As you start programs, they are added to the Active Task List.

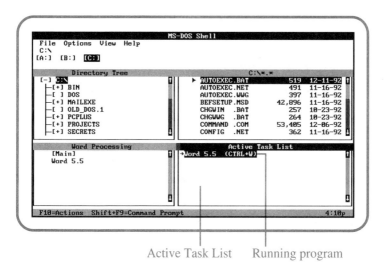

Active Task List   Running program

Figure 16.1   The Active Task List window displays all programs currently running.

To enable task swapping and cause the Active Task List to appear:

Which Way Did It Go?   Do not perform these steps if the Active Task List is showing, or you will turn Task Swapper off.

1. Open the Options menu.

2. Select Enable Task Swapper. (A mark appears in front of the command, indicating that it is on.)

85

Adding Programs to the Active Task List

To add a program to the Active Task List, you start it using any of the methods described in the section, "Selecting a Program to Run." Active programs are added to the Active Task List, as shown in Figure 16.2.

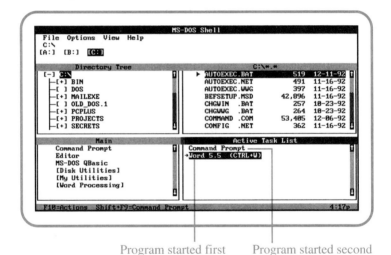

Program started first   Program started second

Figure 16.2   The most recently started program is listed first.

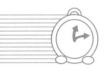

Born to Run   To start a program but remain at the DOS Shell so you can start another one, either press the Shift key as you double-click on the file name, or press and hold the Shift key, select the file name, and press Enter.

You can toggle between active programs and the Shell in a number of ways:

Ctrl+Esc   Returns you to the DOS Shell.

Alt+Tab   Use this repeatedly to cycle through each active application in turn.

Alt+Esc   Takes you to the next application in the Active Task List.

Application shortcut key   Use the shortcut key defined in the Add Program dialog box to jump directly to an application.

Selecting an application from the Active Task List   Jumps you to that application.

Removing Programs from the Active Task List

To remove a program from the Active Task List, you simply exit that program in the usual manner. When a program is no longer active, it is automatically removed from the Active Task List.

In cases of emergency (such as when the application is no longer responding to commands), you may need to shut down a program manually. Follow these steps:

1. Select the program in the Active Task List.

2. Press Del. A warning message appears.

3. Select OK to quit the application.

Backing Up
Your Hard Disk

In this lesson, you will learn how to back up your hard disk.

An Overview of Backup

Not on the Menu? If your Disk Utilities menu does not have an MS Backup command as described in this lesson, modify the Backup Fixed Disk command by selecting the Properties command on the File menu. Change the title and type MSBACKUP in the Commands text box.

A *backup* is a copy of the files on your hard disk. There are three types of backups:

Full backup This backup is a complete copy of every file on your hard disk.

Incremental backup This backup copies only the files that have been changed since the last full or incremental backup. To restore a complete hard disk, you would need *your full backup and all incremental backup diskettes.*

Differential backup   This backup copies only the files that have been changed since the last full backup. A differential backup may take longer than an incremental backup. To restore a complete hard disk, *you would need your full backup and latest differential backup diskettes.*

Here's a Plan   As a rule of thumb, perform a full backup once a month, then perform either an incremental or differential backup at the end of each work day. If you don't perform your full backups often, then use an incremental backup every day, because it won't take as long as a differential backup.

When a backup is performed, a *backup catalog* is created which contains information about what was backed up, and when. The backup catalog is used when restoring files.

To perform a backup, you must select the drives, directories, and the files to be backed up. These selections can be stored permanently in a *setup file*. MS Backup comes with a few setup files already created for common situations, such as a full backup.

The first time you run MS Backup, it will configure itself. To do this, MS Backup will run some tests on your system. You will need two diskettes of the same size and density as the diskettes you will use when you do real backups. Follow the on-screen instructions, and remember to save the configuration when the tests are over.

Performing a Full Backup

To perform a full backup:

To Format or Not to Format   You do not have to have preformatted diskettes to perform a backup; MS Backup will format diskettes as needed. However, using already-formatted diskettes will make the backup process go a lot faster.

1. Open the Disk Utilities menu in the Program List. If the Program List is not displayed on your screen, select Program/File Lists from the View menu.

2. Select MS Backup.

3. Choose Backup. The Backup dialog box, shown in Figure 17.1, appears.

4. In the Backup From box, select the drive to back up. MS Backup will display All Files next to the drive letter you select.

5. Repeat step 4 for additional drives.

6. If you are going to use diskettes of a different type or size from the one listed, change the drive letter in the Backup To box.

7. Select Start Backup.

8. When the backup is complete, press Enter to return to the Shell.

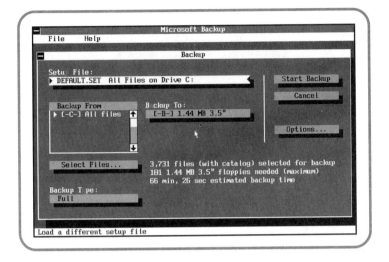

Figure 17.1 You can configure your backup from the Backup dialog box.

 Command Line Users From the DOS prompt, use the command MSBACKUP to start the MS Backup program and back up your hard drive as described in this lesson.

Performing an Incremental or Differential Backup

An incremental backup differs from a differential backup. *Differential* backs up any file that has been changed since the last full backup; *incremental* backs up only those files that have been changed since either a full or an incremental backup (whichever was more recent). Performing an incremental or differential backup of your entire hard disk is easy:

91

1. Open the Disk Utilities menu in the Program List. If the Program List is not displayed on your screen, select Program/File Lists from the View menu.

2. Select MS Backup.

3. Choose Backup. The Backup dialog box appears.

4. In the Backup From box, select the drive to back up. MS Backup will display All Files next to the drive letter you select.

5. Repeat step 4 for additional drives.

6. If you are going to use diskettes of a different type or size from the one listed, change the drive letter in the Backup To box.

7. In the Backup Type box, select Incremental or Differential.

8. Select Start Backup.

9. When the backup is complete, press Enter to return to the Shell.

Backing Up Selected Directories and Files

You may want to back up only certain directories or files. Since all your program files are on the original diskettes, and they don't change, why back them up? By backing up only the directories which contain the files you create, you can reduce the time it takes to do a full backup.

Safety First You may want one full backup of your system (complete with program files) in case of hard drive failure.

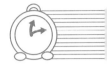

To back up selected directories or files:

1. Open the Disk Utilities menu in the Program List. If the Program List is not displayed on your screen, select Program/File Lists from the **View** menu.

2. Select MS Backup.

3. Choose Backup. The Backup dialog box appears.

4. If you are going to use diskettes of a different type or size from the one listed, change the drive letter in the Backup To box.

5. In the Backup Type box, select Full, Incremental or Differential.

Making a Difference If you want to back up all the files in a selected directory, regardless of when they were last changed, select Full.

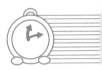

6. If necessary, in the Backup From box, select the drive whose files you want to back up.

7. Choose Select Files, and the Select Backup Files dialog box appears, as shown in Figure 17.2.

8. Select the directories or files to back up.

Make Your Selection, Please An arrow indicates selected directories. If all the files in a directory are not selected, it is displayed with a double arrow. A check mark indicates selected files within a directory.

Unselected directories   Unselected files

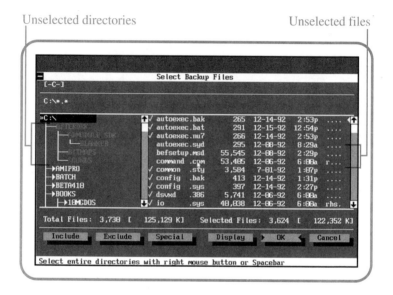

Figure 17.2 Back up selected files and directories with the Select Backup Files dialog box.

With the mouse Double-click (or click with the right mouse button) on a file or directory to select it. To select multiple files or directories, click the left mouse button and hold, click the right mouse button, then drag until the group is selected.

With the keyboard Use the Spacebar to select directories or files.

9. When you are done selecting files, select OK.

10. Select Start Backup.

11. When the backup is complete, press Enter to return to the Shell.

You can also select files by using **Include** and **Exclude** in the Select Backup Files dialog box. Select Include or Exclude, then follow these steps:

1. Enter a directory path, such as C:\WORD\DOCS.

2. Enter a file name pattern, such as *.DOC.

3. Decide whether to include or exclude subdirectories.

4. Select OK.

Using Special in the Select Backup Files dialog box, you can exclude additional files, such as read-only and hidden files.

In this lesson, you learned how to back up your hard disk. In the next lesson, you'll learn how to restore files to your hard disk if they get damaged.

Lesson 18

Restoring Your
Hard Disk

In this lesson, you will learn how to restore your hard disk.

Not on the Menu? If your Disk Utilities menu does not have an MS Backup command, modify the Backup Fixed Disk command as described in the previous lesson. You'll use the same command for backup and restore. Delete the Restore Fixed Disk command.

Restoring a Full Backup

To restore a full backup:

1. Open the Disk Utilities menu in the Program List. If the Program List is not displayed on your screen, select Program/File Lists from the View menu.

2. Select MS Backup.

3. Choose Restore. The Restore dialog box, shown in Figure 18.1, appears.

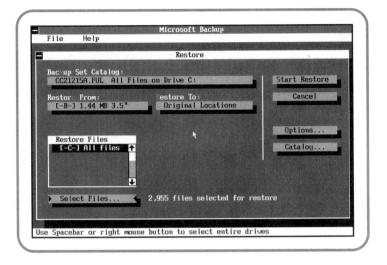

Figure 18.1 You can configure your restoration from the Restore dialog box.

4. In the Restore Files box, select the drive to restore. Use the drive that the files were backed up from, regardless of whether you want to restore the files to a different drive. All Files will display next to the drive letter you select.

5. Repeat step 4 for additional drives.

6. If you are going to use diskettes of a different type or size from the one listed, change the drive letter in the Restore From box.

7. If you want to restore files to different drives or directories from which they were backed up, select Restore To.

8. Select Start Restore.

9. When the restore is complete, press Enter to return to the Shell.

C> Command Line Users From the DOS prompt, use the command MSBACKUP to start the MS Backup program and restore files to your hard drive as described in this lesson.

Restoring Selected Directories and Files

You may want to restore only certain directories or files. By restoring only the files or directories you need, you can reduce the time it takes to do a full restore.

To restore selected directories or files:

1. Open the Disk Utilities menu in the Program List. If the Program List is not displayed on your screen, select Program/File Lists from the View menu.

2. Select MS Backup.

3. Choose Restore. The Restore dialog box appears.

4. If you are going to use diskettes of a different type or size from the one listed, change the drive letter in the Restore From box.

5. If necessary, in the Restore Files box, select the drive whose files you want to restore. Use the drive that the files were backed up from, regardless of whether you want to restore the files to a different drive.

6. Choose Select Files, and the Select Restore Files dialog box appears, as shown in Figure 18.2.

Selected files

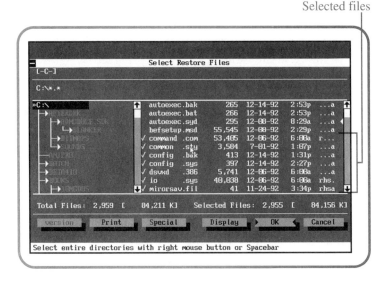

Figure 18.2 Restore selected files and directories with the Select Restore Files dialog box.

7. Select the directories or files to restore:

Make Your Selection, Please Selected directories display with an arrow. If all the files in a directory are not selected, it is displayed with a double arrow. Selected files within it display with a check mark.

With the mouse Double-click (or click with the right mouse button) on a file or directory to select it. To select multiple files or directories, click the left mouse button and hold, click the right mouse button, then drag until the group is selected. To select noncontiguous files or directories, press Ctrl and click on each item.

With the keyboard   Use the Spacebar to select directories or files.

8. When you are done selecting files, select OK.

9. If you want to restore files to different drives or directories from which they were backed up, select Restore To.

10. Select Start Restore.

11. When the restore is complete, press Enter to return to the Shell.

If more than one version of a file exists on your different backup sets, the most recent version is the one DOS restores. You can select a different version by using Version from the Select Restore Files dialog box.

Using Special in the Select Restore Files dialog box, you can exclude additional files from restoration, such as system and hidden files.

In this lesson, you learned how to restore files if they become damaged. In the next lesson, you will learn how to keep your system safe from viruses.

Lesson 19

Keeping Your System Safe from Viruses

In this lesson, you will learn how to detect and remove computer viruses.

What Is a Computer Virus?

A *virus* is a program that infects your computer in various ways, such as changing your files, damaging your disks, and preventing your computer from starting.

You can infect your system any time you copy or download files onto your disk, or boot from a diskette. You can protect yourself from serious damage by:

- Maintaining a recent backup of your files.

- Checking diskettes for viruses before copying files from them. *Be sure to check program disks before installing new software.*

- Write-protecting program diskettes to prevent infection.

- Running VSafe, a special DOS 6 virus-detection program, all the time.

- Never starting your computer with a diskette in the drive. (Make a virus-free bootable diskette for emergency purposes—see the next section.)

- Running Microsoft Anti-Virus (another DOS 6 program) as soon as a problem occurs.

Creating a Startup Diskette

You can create a virus-safe startup diskette by following the instructions in Lesson 13. After the diskette is formatted, add the following files:

- CONFIG.SYS

- AUTOEXEC.BAT

- MSAV.EXE

- MSAV.HLP

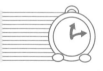 **Current Affair** Keep your system files current by copying your CONFIG.SYS and AUTOEXEC.BAT files onto your emergency-startup diskette whenever you modify them.

After you've copied these files onto the diskette, write-protect it to prevent infection. If you ever need the diskette, you'll have a good copy of your system files and the virus-detection program.

Scanning for Viruses

If you suspect a virus, follow these steps immediately to scan your disk:

1. Exit all programs, including the DOS Shell.

2. Boot your system with your startup diskette.

3. At the DOS prompt, type msav /A /C and press Enter. (If you are connected to a network, type MSAV /L /C. This will limit scanning to local drives only.) The Anti-Virus Main Menu appears, as shown in Figure 19.1. All local drives are scanned and cleaned of any viruses found.

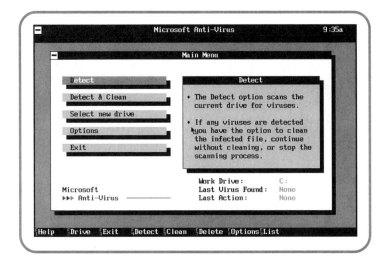

Figure 19.1   Select scanning options from the Anti-Virus screen.

4. After the scan is complete, press F3 to exit.

 **Stop That Scan!** You can stop the scan process at any time by pressing F3.

If you prefer to control the virus scanning manually, type MSAV at the prompt. From the Anti-Virus Main Menu, select from among these options:

- If necessary, press F2 or choose Select new drive to change the drive you want to check for viruses.

- Press F8 or choose Options to change various scanning options, such as disabling the alarm sound and creating a report of the virus scan.

- Start the scan by selecting either Detect (F4) or Detect & Clean (F5). If you choose **D**etect, you will be able to select a course of action if an infected file is detected.

 **Keeping Up with the Times** New viruses are invented every day. Keep your virus detection current by updating the list of viruses. See your DOS manual for more details.

Performing Virus Scans Automatically at Startup

To perform a scan of your hard disk every time you boot your computer, add the following command to your AUTOEXEC.BAT file (for more information on editing your AUTOEXEC.BAT file, see Lesson 23):

```
MSAV /N
```

If you are attached to a network, use this command instead:

MSAV /N /L

With one of these commands in place, your hard disk will be scanned automatically at startup. If any viruses are detected, a dialog box will appear, offering several options:

* Choose Clean to clean the virus from your system.

* Choose Continue to ignore the virus, but continue scanning. If you know that a file was changed legitimately, use this option.

* Choose Stop to stop the scanning process and go to the Anti-Virus Main Menu.

* Choose Delete to delete the infected file from your system. Use this option if the file has been destroyed by a virus, and you wish to prevent further infection.

Using the MSAV command at startup will detect only viruses that are active at that time. To have ongoing protection, run VSafe. VSafe is a program that runs in the background as you perform your normal computer tasks. VSafe will warn you of changes to your files that might be caused by viruses. To start VSafe automatically every time you boot your computer, add this command to your AUTOEXEC.BAT (for more information on editing your AUTOEXEC.BAT file, see Lesson 23):

VSAFE

In this lesson you learned how to detect and prevent viruses. In the next lesson, you will learn how to double your hard disk space with DoubleSpace.

Doubling Your Disk Space with DoubleSpace

In this lesson, you will learn how to double your hard disk space.

What Is a Compressed Drive?

Disk compression programs such as DoubleSpace can store more information on a disk because data is stored more densely than with MS-DOS alone. If you use DoubleSpace, your hard disk can increase its capacity by almost two times.

When you install DOS 6, your drives are still uncompressed. You must run DoubleSpace to compress a drive. After you install DoubleSpace, your hard disk will consist of two sections, as shown in Figure 20.1. One section will remain uncompressed, to support the few programs and system files that cannot run on a compressed drive.

You can use a drive compressed with DoubleSpace the same way you use any regular drive; the only difference is that it will store more files than it normally would. Unbelievable? The next section explains how it's done.

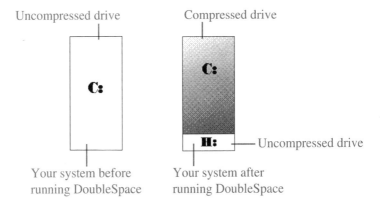

Uncompressed drive · Compressed drive

C:

C:

H: —— Uncompressed drive

Your system before running DoubleSpace · Your system after running DoubleSpace

Figure 20.1 Before and after DoubleSpace installation.

Check Those Utilities If you depend on third-party utilities such as PC Tools and Norton Utilities, make sure that they are compatible with a DoubleSpace drive. If you're not sure, consult the manual or call the manufacturer before you run these programs.

How DoubleSpace Works

If you don't care about how DoubleSpace works (but are simply grateful that it does), you can skip this part.

After DoubleSpace installation, your physical drive C is unaltered. But there is a huge file that takes up most of it now. This huge file, called *DBLSPACE.000*, is your compressed drive. DOS assigns a drive letter to this file, so you can access your files from it.

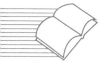

Most Illogical The DBLSPACE.000 file is not really a drive. DOS pretends that it is, so the files within it can be read normally. A drive that is not physically a drive is called a *logical drive*.

All the files that were formerly on your hard disk are compressed into DBLSPACE.000, along with most of the free space remaining on the drive. A little bit of free space is left outside of DBLSPACE.000 (uncompressed) in case you need it.

Here's the tricky part. DOS knows that you expect all the files that were on C: before to be accessible from C: now. So it assigns the drive letter C to the *compressed* drive, and changes the name of the *real* drive C to something else (usually H: or I:). That way you can still do everything from the C: prompt like you did before you compressed your hard disk.

Using DoubleSpace to Compress a Drive

There's No Looking Back Once you compress a drive, you can shrink its size, but you can't reverse the compression process. If you try to do this by deleting the DBLSPACE.000 file, you'll lose everything that was on the compressed drive. As a safety precaution, do a full backup before running DoubleSpace (see Lesson 17).

It takes roughly 1 minute per megabyte of data to compress your hard disk, so you might want to start the

DoubleSpace setup program at the end of the day, and run it overnight. To set up DoubleSpace, follow these steps:

1. Exit all programs, including the DOS Shell.

2. Change to the DOS directory by typing `CD\DOS` and pressing Enter.

3. Start the DoubleSpace setup program by typing `DBLSPACE` and pressing Enter. To exit at any time, press F3.

4. Choose between Custom or Express setup. (Unless you are an experienced user, select Express setup.) If you'd like to run Custom setup to compress a drive other than C: or to create an empty compressed drive, press F1 to obtain more information.

5. A small section of your drive will remain uncompressed. If you want to change the default letter for the uncompressed drive, do so before pressing Enter.

6. A message will appear which tells you how long the compression process will take. This one-time process takes about 1 minute per megabyte. Press C to Continue (which will complete the compression process) or Esc to exit (which will stop it).

7. After the disk compression is finished, a summary will display, showing information on the compressed drive. Press Enter and your system will restart with the compressed drive active.

Here's Looking at You, Kid   Typing `DIR /C` will display information about a compressed drive.

Now That I Have a Compressed Drive, What Do I Do with It?

Work with your compressed drive as you would with any other drive. The compression process remains invisible to you, the user. The DoubleSpace maintenance program allows you to perform these compression functions:

- Increase the storage capacity of diskettes by compressing them.

- Adjust the size of your compressed drive.

- Display information about the compressed drive.

- Format a compressed drive.

- Defragment a compressed drive.

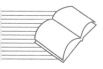 **Defragmentation** When a file is placed on a drive, parts of the file may be split over different sections of the drive in order to make the most effective use of available space. On an uncompressed drive, fragmentation can cause a drop in speed when accessing files. Defragmenting a drive causes the parts of files that were split up to be placed together. Defragmenting a compressed drive may not affect speed as much as on an uncompressed drive, but it will usually result in additional space on the drive.

- Check a compressed drive's integrity.

Access the DoubleSpace maintenance program by typing DBLSPACE at the DOS prompt.

Compressing a Diskette

You can use DoubleSpace to increase the storage capacity of your diskettes. After a diskette has been compressed by DoubleSpace, it becomes immediately available for copying files, etc. If you remove the diskette or reboot, you will need to use the Mount command to make the diskette available (details are covered later).

Compression Depression You can only use a compressed diskette on a PC that uses DOS 6, and is running DoubleSpace.

You can only compress a diskette if you have already run the DoubleSpace setup program. To compress a diskette:

1. Insert the diskette in its drive.

2. At the DOS prompt, type DBLSPACE and press Enter.

3. Open the Compress menu.

4. Select the Existing Drive command. The dialog box shown in Figure 20.2 is displayed. Press Enter.

5. Return to DOS by selecting the Exit command from the Drive menu.

6. Now that the diskette has been compressed, use the diskette as you would any other—*but while you are using it, do not remove it from its drive or reboot.*

111

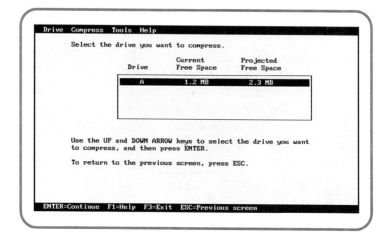

Figure 20.2 Compressing a diskette is easy.

If you need to mount a compressed diskette in order to use it, follow these steps:

1. Place the diskette in its drive.

2. At the DOS prompt, type `DBLSPACE` and press Enter.

3. Open the Drive menu.

4. Select the Mount command.

5. Return to DOS by selecting the Exit command from the Drive menu.

6. Now that the diskette has been mounted, use the diskette as you would any other—*but while you are using it, do not remove it from its drive or reboot.*

Lesson 21

Making the Most of Your System's Memory

In this lesson, you will learn how to optimize your system's memory.

What Is Memory?

Your computer comes with two kinds of memory: RAM (random access memory) and ROM (read-only memory). ROM stores the permanent instructions your computer needs to operate. RAM is a temporary storage area used by your programs.

When you start a program, it is loaded into RAM and it starts executing instructions. As you work on a letter or some other file, that file is kept in RAM so changes can be made. If you create large documents, your program requires large amounts of RAM to manipulate the information in the document. Your program loads other files into RAM as needed—if you spell-check your letter, for example, the spell-check program is loaded into memory where the main program can use it.

All programs need memory in order to run—some need quite a lot of memory. Not having enough memory can affect the way your programs work—and even prevent some programs from starting. It is vital that you make the most of the memory your computer has.

How Much Memory Does Your Computer Have?

Memory is divided into *bytes*. A byte stores a single character, such as the letter Q. A *kilobyte* (1K) is roughly 1,000 bytes (it's really 1,024 bytes.) A *megabyte* (1MB) is roughly 1,000,000 bytes (it's really 1,048,576 bytes.) RAM is divided into several areas:

Conventional memory The first 640K of RAM. Conventional is the most important area of memory because it's the only one in which a program can run.

Upper memory Memory above 640K and below 1MB. Usually this area is reserved for your system's use, but pockets of unused space (called *upper memory blocks*) can be converted for use by device drivers and memory-resident (TSRs, or terminate-and-stay-resident) programs.

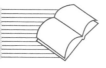

Memory-Resident Programs Also known as TSRs or terminate-and-stay-resident programs. These are programs (like VSafe) which load into memory and "go to sleep" until something activates them.

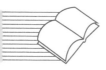

Device Driver A special program that controls optional devices, such as a mouse or a network card.

Extended memory Memory above 1MB; it is used to store data temporarily. It cannot be used to run programs. Only certain special programs (such as Windows, DESQview, and AutoCAD) can use this area of memory. Programs such as these access extended memory not through DOS, but through a special extended-memory manager, such as EMM386.EXE (which comes with DOS 5 and 6.) The ability to access extended memory through an extended-memory *manager* must be written into an application specifically—otherwise, that program will not use extended memory, even if you load EMM386.EXE.

Upper memory The first 64K of extended memory. With the help of an upper-memory manager such as HIMEM.SYS, DOS can access this area of extended memory directly. Upper memory is a good place to store device drivers, memory resident programs, or even DOS itself.

Expanded memory Special memory that is linked to DOS through a window in upper memory. As with extended memory, programs can use expanded memory only indirectly—through the use of an expanded memory manager—and it is much slower than extended memory.

Memory Imposter Extended memory can sometimes be made to simulate expanded memory. You would want to do this if you had a program which needed expanded memory and not extended memory. Although expanded memory simulated in this manner would occupy the same physical space as extended memory, the method that a program uses to access that memory is quite different (via a different memory manager) so if you convert part of your system's extended memory into expanded memory, only programs which use expanded memory can access that section of RAM.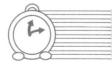

115

To see how much memory your system has (and of what type), follow these steps:

1. Select Command Prompt in the Program List or press Shift+F9.

2. Type MEM and press Enter. A listing similar to Figure 21.1 will appear. From this listing, you can determine the amount of each kind of memory being used (Adapter RAM/ROM is memory located on add-on boards such as video boards.)

```
C:\>mem

Memory Type        Total =  Used  +  Free
---------------    ------   ------    ------
Conventional        640K      45K      595K
Upper                91K      64K       27K
Adapter RAM/ROM     293K     293K        0K
Extended (XMS)*    3072K     576K     2496K
                   ------    ------    ------
Total memory       4096K     978K     3118K

Total under 1 MB    731K     109K      622K

*   1024K of XMS memory is configured for XMS/EMS sharing.
     480K of this amount is in use as EMS.
     544K is available for either XMS or EMS.

Total Expanded (EMS)              1408K (1441792 bytes)
Free Expanded (EMS)                928K  (950272 bytes)
Largest executable program size    595K  (609568 bytes)
Largest free upper memory block     27K   (27552 bytes)
MS-DOS is resident in the high memory area.

C:\>
```

Figure 21.1 Seeing how much memory your system has.

To display a listing of programs (shown in Figure 21.2) currently loaded into memory:

1. Select Command Prompt in the Program List or press Shift+F9.

2. Type MEM /C /P. (The /P switch tells the MEM command to list only one screen's worth of information at a time.)

3. To see the next screen-full of information, press Enter.

4. Type EXIT to return to the Shell.

```
Modules using memory below 1 MB:

  Name           Total      =   Conventional  +   Upper Memory
  ---------------------------------------------------------------
  MSDOS          16653  (16K)      16653  (16K)        0    (0K)
  HIMEM           1104   (1K)       1104   (1K)        0    (0K)
  EMM386          4144   (4K)       4144   (4K)        0    (0K)
  SMARTDRV        2400   (2K)       2400   (2K)        0    (0K)
  COMMAND         2912   (3K)       2912   (3K)        0    (0K)
  SAVE            9200   (9K)       9200   (9K)        0    (0K)
  DOSSHELL        2288   (2K)       2288   (2K)        0    (0K)
  COMMAND         3504   (3K)       3504   (3K)        0    (0K)
  COMMAND         3136   (3K)       3136   (3K)        0    (0K)
  MOUSE          17296  (17K)          0   (0K)    17296  (17K)
  ANSI            4208   (4K)          0   (0K)     4208   (4K)
  DBLSPACE       44272  (43K)          0   (0K)    44272  (43K)
  Free          637216 (622K)     609664 (595K)    27552  (27K)

Memory Summary:

  Type of Memory        Total      =     Used      +      Free
  ---------------------------------------------------------------
  Conventional         655360 (640K)    45696  (45K)    609664 (595K)
Press any key to continue . . .
```

Figure 21.2   Which programs are using memory?

Maximizing Memory with MemMaker

MemMaker is a diagnostic program that comes with DOS 6. MemMaker is designed to optimize the way your system uses memory by changing your configuration files. In order to use MemMaker, you must have a 386 or 486 processor and extended memory.

Expecting Miracles?   MemMaker is great, but it's not perfect. You can optimize your system's memory usage beyond what MemMaker can do for you. If you want to know more about memory and how to make the most of it, read *10 Minute Guide to Memory Management*.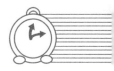

117

MemMaker is very easy to use, and it provides fairly good results. To optimize your system with MemMaker:

1. Exit all programs, including the DOS Shell.

2. At the DOS prompt, type MEMMAKER and press Enter. A screen appears, welcoming you to MemMaker.

3. Press Enter and a message appears, asking you to choose between Express (the easiest) and Custom (for confident users) optimization. To use Express, press Enter. To switch to Custom, press the Spacebar, then Enter. The Express option works well for most systems. If you are an advanced user with a good understanding of memory management, you can use Custom optimization to free up a bit more memory. If you use Custom optimization and need additional help, press F1 at any time.

4. A message appears, asking you if you use any programs that require expanded memory. Press Y for Yes, or N for No. Press Enter to continue.

Expanding Your Horizons If you are not sure whether or not your programs need expanded memory, check the owners' manual. If a program requires expanded memory, it will be clearly marked. If you're in doubt, answer no. If a program won't start and it says it needs expanded memory, then rerun MemMaker and answer yes.

5. Press Enter, and MemMaker will reboot your computer and verify your configuration.

6. MemMaker makes changes to your AUTOEXEC.BAT and CONFIG.SYS (your old files are saved with a .UMB extension.) Press Enter, and MemMaker will test your new configuration.

MemMaker Blues? If your system locks up (freezes) while MemMaker is testing, you can reboot your system and MemMaker will pick up where it left off. To reboot, press Ctrl, Alt, and Delete at the same time.

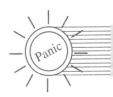

7. Wait until a message appears, asking whether your new configuration is OK. Press Y for Yes or N for No. Press Enter to continue.

8. If there is a problem, MemMaker can undo its changes, or allow you to do further testing. Press Enter to undo changes (MemMaker will ask you to confirm), or press the Spacebar and then Enter to keep the changes.

9. A listing showing your system's memory usage appears. Press Enter to exit MemMaker.

Memories... To undo the changes made by MemMaker at any time, type MEMMAKER /UNDO and press Enter.

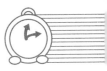

In this lesson, you learned how to maximize your memory with MemMaker. In the next lesson, you will learn how to use DOS 6 with a network.

119

MS-DOS 6 and Your Laptop Computer

In this lesson, you will learn how to use DOS 6 with your laptop computer.

Connecting Your Laptop with Another Computer

Through a program called Interlink, you can connect your laptop to another computer, upload files, download files, and print documents. Suppose you work as an account representative, taking orders on the road. When you return to the office, you can download new client information and sales orders to your office computer. You can even "borrow" your office printer to print sales reports.

As shown in Figure 23.1, once the connection is made, the laptop becomes the *client* (because it uses resources), and the office computer becomes the *server* (because it provides resources). You access the drives on the office computer as if they were additional drives on your laptop. In this example, if you copied files from your laptop to drive D, you would actually be copying the files to drive A of the office computer. In this example, drive E on the laptop equals drive B on the office computer, and the laptop's drive F equals drive C.

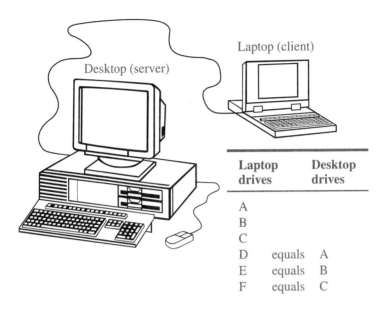

Figure 23.1 Linking two computers together.

To use Interlink, you need the following:

- Either a 3-wire *serial cable*, a 7-wire *null modem cable*, or a *bidirectional printer cable* (if you're not sure what these are, consult your computer dealer). Connect the cable to the appropriate port at the back of each computer. Depending on the type of cable you are using, you'll connect either a serial port on one PC to a serial port on the other, or a parallel port to a parallel port.

- MS-DOS version 6.0 on the server, and 3.0 or higher on the client computer.

- Free conventional memory—16K on the client (the laptop), and 130K on the server (the office computer).

Setting Up the Client

Follow these steps to set up the client:

1. If necessary, copy INTERLNK.EXE to the \DOS directory. If the client PC uses DOS 6, the INTERLNK.EXE file will already be there. If not, copy it from the server PC's \DOS directory.

2. Add the following to your CONFIG.SYS (for more information about editing your CONFIG.SYS file, see Lesson 23):

```
DEVICE=C:\DOS\INTERLNK.EXE
```

   If you need to use more than 3 drives on the server, add a /DRIVES:*n* switch. For example, to use 4 drives:

```
DEVICE=C:\DOS\INTERLNK.EXE /DRIVES:4
```

3. Restart the client computer.

I'll Be Your Server   There is nothing you need to do to set up the server computer. The necessary files are located in the \DOS directory already, and no changes need to be made to the configuration files.

Establishing a Connection

To establish the connection between the client and the server, follow these steps:

1. Verify that the client is set up.

2. Connect the client and the server with one of the recommended cables.

3. On the server, type the following (press Enter at the end of each command):

```
CD\DOS
INTERSRV
```

4. Reboot the client. You should see a listing like this:

```
Microsoft Interlink version 1.00

Port=LPT1
Drive letters redirected: 3 (D: through F:)
Printer ports redirected: 2 (LPT1: through
LPT2:)

This Computer     Other Computer
  (Client)          (Server)
_____  _____
    D:    equals    A:
    E:    equals    B:
    F:    equals    C:(120 Mb) MS-DOS_6
    LPT1: equals    LPT2:
    LPT2: equals    LPT3:
```

Now you can copy files. Just remember to use the correct drive letter when referring to the server's drives. When you want to break the connection, press Alt+F4 on the server's keyboard.

Using DOS to Conserve Your Laptop's Power

DOS 6 comes with a program called Power, which can help you conserve power on your laptop during times when applications or devices are idle. Your power savings can be as high as 25%!

To use the Power program:

1. Add the following to your CONFIG.SYS (for more information about editing your CONFIG.SYS file, see Lesson 23):

```
DEVICE=C:\DOS\POWER.EXE
```

2. Reboot your laptop.

To display the current power setting, type POWER and press Enter.

In this lesson, you learned how to establish a link between two computers for sharing files and printers. You also learned how to conserve power on a laptop computer. In the next lesson, you will learn how to edit your AUTOEXEC.BAT and CONFIG.SYS files.

Lesson 23
Editing a File with the DOS Editor

In this lesson, you will learn how to edit text files such as CONFIG.SYS and AUTOEXEC.BAT using the DOS 6 editor.

A Word Before You Edit

When you edit your configuration files, keep these things in mind:

- Do not edit CONFIG.SYS or AUTOEXEC.BAT without a startup diskette handy. Instructions for making a boot-startup diskette are covered in Lesson 13 and Lesson 19.

- If you make changes to a configuration file, make sure you reboot your PC to make those changes effective.

Copy Cat! It is a good practice to make a copy of your original file before you start editing. Follow the procedures outlined in Lesson 8 to keep current copies of your CONFIG.SYS and AUTOEXEC.BAT files on your boot diskette.

Using the DOS 6 Editor

An easy-to-use, full-screen text editor called EDIT (the DOS Editor) comes with DOS 6. Although it is beyond the scope of this book to teach you everything you might need to know about using EDIT, this lesson will teach you enough to edit simple files such as CONFIG.SYS and AUTOEXEC.BAT.

Getting Down to BASICs The DOS Editor is a QBASIC-driven program. QBASIC is installed in the DOS directory during installation. Do not delete the QBASIC files, or the DOS Editor will not work.

Starting the DOS 6 Editor

Follow these steps to start the DOS 6 Editor from the Dos Shell:

1. Change to the directory which holds the file you want to edit. (To edit CONFIG.SYS or AUTOEXEC.BAT, change to the root directory.)

2. Select Editor from the Program List.

3. Type the name of the file you want to edit. The file you requested is opened as Figure 23.1 shows.

Command Line Users The equivalent DOS command for starting the Editor is EDIT.

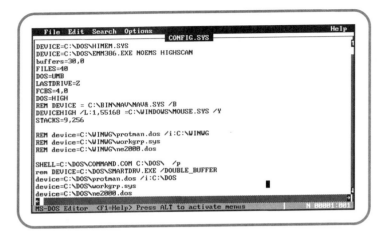

Figure 23.1   The CONFIG.SYS file is ready to edit.

Making Changes

Once a file is open, you can make changes to it. Although there are many ways to move around the screen, the most commonly used methods are those shown in Table 23.1:

Table 23.1   Moving around the DOS 6 Editor.

To move:	Press:
Up, down, left, or right	Arrow keys
To the beginning of a line	Home key
To the end of a line	End key
To the beginning of the next line	Ctrl+Enter
To the top of the window	Ctrl+Q, then E
To the bottom of the window	Ctrl+Q, then X

When you start the DOS 6 Editor, you are in *Insert mode*. That means when you position your cursor and start to type, what you type is inserted at that point. If you want to type over existing characters, press the Insert key. You are now in *Overtype mode*. Change back to Insert mode by pressing Insert again.

If you want to delete some characters, position your cursor on any character, and use the Delete key.

To insert a blank line before the line the cursor is on, position your cursor at the beginning of an existing line and press Enter.

Saving Your File

After making changes to your file, you must save it before exiting the Editor. To save your changes:

1. Open the File menu.

2. Select the Save command.

3. If you want to keep your original file intact (without changes) and save this file under a new name, press A from the File menu or click on the Save As command. Type the new file name and press Enter.

Exiting the DOS 6 Editor

After you have saved your changes, you can safely exit the Editor.

1. Open the File menu.

2. Select the Exit command. You will be returned to the DOS Shell.

Made a Mistake? If you decide after making changes to a file, that you do not want to save those changes, simply exit the Editor without saving.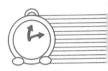

In this lesson, you learned how to use the DOS 6 Editor. This is the last lesson. For your convenience, Appendixes A and B provide instructions for entering commands at the DOS prompt. Appendix C provides a summary of what's new in DOS 6.

Overtime

Using the DOS Prompt to Enter Commands

Although the DOS Shell is easier to use (especially for beginners), occasionally you may want to enter DOS commands at the DOS prompt.

Entering DOS Commands

The *DOS prompt* is the on-screen marker that beckons you to enter a command. When you type a command, it appears after the prompt. The DOS prompt normally appears as the following:

```
C>
```

Since this type of prompt is not very informative, many people change the DOS prompt display so that it shows the current drive and directory, as in:

```
C:\DOS>
```

The Informer   If your prompt looks like `c>`, but you want it to display the directory, type PROMPT `$P$G` and press Enter. To make this change permanent, add this command to your AUTOEXEC.BAT. See Lesson 23 for more information.

131

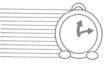

Promptness Don't make the mistake that a lot of beginners do—which is typing the prompt, then the command. If you see a DOS command in a book (such as this one) which is displayed as:

`C:\DOS>FORMAT A:`

You should type only `FORMAT A:`. The rest is simply a prompt that you will see every time you press Enter.

DOS Command Syntax

Some DOS commands have *parameters*, which tell DOS what file or other object to act upon. For example, the DEL command is used to delete a file. The parameter you use with the DEL command is the name of the file you want deleted, as in `DEL DUMBFILE.DOC`.

Some commands have additional options, called *switches*, that you enter after the command. For example, to see what programs are in memory, you enter `MEM /C`. Switches are entered with a forward slash (/). You can use as many switches as you want. For example, to display the programs in memory, one screenful at a time, you enter `MEM /C /P`.

To summarize—DOS commands can be made up of several elements:

The command itself For example, `FORMAT`.

Optional parameters which explain what drives or files to act on For example, `A:`.

Optional switches which allow a single command to act in a variety of ways For example, /F:360.

The completed command could look like this:

FORMAT A: /F:360

The Path to Success

In order to specify a file to be used with a command, you need to give its complete path. Otherwise, DOS might get confused when it tries to locate the file you want the command to affect. The path for a file consists of its

Drive A drive designation is made up of the drive letter, followed by a colon (which indicates that you are talking about a disk drive). For example, if a file is located on drive C, then C: would be the first part of that file's path.

Directory path A directory path is made up of a backslash (\) followed by the name of the directory, followed by another backslash. A subdirectory is indicated by entering the name of the subdirectory, followed by another backslash. For example, if you had a file in a directory called DOCS, which is a subdirectory of WORD, the directory path would be \WORD\DOCS\.

File name This part is easy—it's the name of the file, as in BUDGET.DOC.

The completed path would look like this:

C:\WORD\DOCS\BUDGET.DOC

File Finder Since directory names do not usually include extensions, when you see the part of a file path that has an extension, it is probably a file name. For example, in the path:

C:\PROJECTS\TDG\ORIG\CHAP01.DOC

the file name is obviously CHAP01.DOC, because that's the only thing with an extension (.DOC).

Oh, My Tired Fingers! Don't use the complete path for a file name unless you have to. If the file you are trying to use is located in the current directory, just type the file name, and DOS will know what you mean.

External Versus Internal Commands

One thing makes DOS commands a headache: some commands are *internal*—loaded into memory at startup (therefore ready to go)—and others are not.

When working with an *external* command, change to the DOS directory first. DOS won't know what the command is unless it can find it. (External DOS commands are stored in the DOS directory; by going there, DOS will recognize the command when you type it in.) A DOS external command is just like any other program—DOS can only find it if it's in the current directory. You can add a path in front of the command, as in:

```
C:\DOS\FORMAT A:
```

But that's no fun—and it's downright confusing. Want to forget all this business about internal and external commands? Just make sure your AUTOEXEC.BAT file contains something like this (refer to Lesson 23 for instructions on how to edit your AUTOEXEC.BAT):

```
PATH=C:\DOS
```

The PATH command tells DOS to look for its external commands in the \DOS directory, so you don't have to enter a path every time you use a command. With this PATH statement in your AUTOEXEC.BAT, you could enter just this, and DOS would know what you mean:

```
FORMAT A:
```

Paths to Other Places You can include other directories in the PATH statement too, so that you can start your programs from any directory. (PATH finds only program files, not data files.) Just separate the directory names by semicolons. For example, my path looks like this: `PATH=C:\DOS;C:\WINDOWS;C:\WP51;C:\WORD`. As another tip, place the directories you use the most at the front of your path—since I use DOS and Windows the most, they are at the front of my path.

How to Interpret DOS Command Syntax

Every book will list DOS *command syntax* (a line which shows how to enter a command) using its own set of rules, but most books use the following conventions:

What you type exactly as shown is capitalized. Even though it makes no difference whether you use upper- or lowercase letters when you enter DOS commands, they are usually displayed in all caps.

Things for which you must substitute a real name are shown in italics. For example, if a command requires you to enter the name of a file, it will be shown as *filename.ext*. Don't type the word FILENAME.EXT; instead, type the actual name of the file, such as TAX93.WKS.

Optional stuff is placed in square brackets. Square brackets [and] will surround a command's options. You don't need to use them unless they fit your situation.

Switches are displayed with a forward slash. For example, the page switch for the MEM command would be shown as [/P]. (Remember, the brackets indicate that the page switch is optional.)

A sample command syntax could look like this:

DEL [*d:*][*path*]*filename.ext*

The actual command you type—keeping in mind that brackets indicate options, and italics indicate where you substitute real information—could look like this:

DEL STUPID.DOC

or

DEL C:\WEIRD\STUPID.DOC

Appendix B

DOS Command Reference

This appendix briefly describes the DOS commands used most often. For more information about a particular command, type HELP *command* at the DOS prompt. If you're not sure how to enter DOS commands at the prompt, or how to read DOS syntax, refer to Appendix A for more information.

CD (CHDIR)

Displays or changes the active directory.

    CD [*d*:][*path*]

Example: CD\WORD

CHKDSK

Displays available disk and memory space, and (optional) corrects disk errors.

    CHKDSK [*d*:] [/F]

Switches:

/F   Causes CHKDSK to fix any errors it finds.

Example: CHKDSK C: /F

CLS

Clears your screen.

    CLS

COPY

Copies files to a directory or disk.

    COPY [d:][path]source.ext [d:][path][destination.ext]

Example: COPY C:\AUTOEXEC.BAT A:

DBLSPACE

Accesses the DoubleSpace maintenance program which can be used to compress a drive or a diskette. Can also be used to mount a compressed diskette for use.

    DBLSPACE [/MOUNT drive:]

Example: DBLSPACE or

DBLSPACE /MOUNT A:

DEL

Deletes files.

    DEL [d:][path]filename.ext [/P]

Switches:

/P Asks for confirmation before deleting a file.

Example: DEL *.* /P

DELTREE

Deletes a directory and its subdirectories.

```
DELTREE [/Y][d:]path
```

Switches:

/Y Deletes the directory tree without first prompting you to confirm.

Example: DELTREE C:\WORD\ JUNK

DIR

Lists files in the specified directory.

```
DIR [d:][path][filename.ext] [/P][/W][/
A:attributes][/O:sortorder]
[/S][/B][/L][/C][/CH]
```

Switches:

/P Lists files one screen at time.

/W Lists files across the screen.

/A Lists files with selected attributes.

/O Lists files in the selected order.

/S Lists files in subdirectories too.

/B Lists files with no heading.

/L Lists files in lowercase.

/C Displays disk compression information, using a default 8K cluster size.

/CH Displays disk compression information, using the cluster size of the host computer.

Example: DIR /P

DISKCOPY

Copies a diskette.

```
DISKCOPY sourcedisk: destinationdisk:
```

Example: DISKCOPY A: A:

DOSSHELL

Starts the DOS Shell.

```
DOSSHELL
```

EDIT

Starts the DOS Editor and (optional) loads a file to edit.

```
EDIT [d:][path][filename.ext]
```

Example: EDIT C:\AUTOEXEC.BAT

EXIT

Returns you to the DOS Shell from the DOS command prompt.

```
EXIT
```

FORMAT

Prepares a diskette for use.

```
FORMAT d: [/S][F:size][/Q][/U][V:label][/B]
```

Switches:

/S Creates a bootable diskette.

/F Formats to the specified *size*.

/Q Performs a quick format.

/U Performs an unconditional format.

/V Adds a volume *label* to the formatted disk.

/B Allocates space for system files, but does not copy them.

Example: FORMAT A:

HELP
Accesses the DOS help system.

```
HELP [command]
```

MAIL
Accesses the Microsoft Mail electronic mail system.

```
MAIL
```

MD (MKDIR)
Creates a directory.

```
MD [d:]path
```

Example: MD C:\WORD\DOCS

MEM
Displays available memory.

```
MEM [/P][/C]
```

Switches:

/P Displays one screen-full at a time.

/C Displays the programs in memory.

Example: MEM /P /C

MEMMAKER

Runs MemMaker, a program which automatically configures your system for best memory usage.

```
MEMMAKER
```

MOVE

Moves files to the location you specify. Also used to rename directories.

```
MOVE [d:][originalpath]filename.ext
[d:]destinationpath[filename.ext]
```

Example: MOVE C:\OLDSUB C:\NEWSUB

or

MOVE C:\MKTG\JFSALES.DOC
D:\SALES\DSSALES.DOC

MSAV

Runs Microsoft Anti-Virus, which checks the indicated drives for existing viruses, and optionally removes them.

```
MSAV [d:] [/C] [/A] [/L] [/N]
```

Switches:

/C Removes any viruses it finds.

/A Scans all drives but A: and B:.

/L Scans only local drives, not network drives.

/N Scans for viruses while not displaying the normal interface. Use this switch at startup.

Example: MSAV /A /C

MSBACKUP

Starts MS Backup, which you can use to back up or restore your hard disk or selected directories or files.

```
MSBACKUP
```

PROMPT

Customizes the DOS prompt.

```
PROMPT [$P][$G][$D][$T][text]
```

Options:

$P   Displays current directory path.

$G   Displays the greater-than sign.

$D   Displays the current date.

$T   Displays the current time.

text Displays the indicated text.

Example: PROMPT $P *Enter your command here*$G

RD (RMDIR)

Removes a directory if it's empty of files.

```
RD [d:]path
```

Example: RD \PROGRAMS\JUNK

REN

Renames a file.

REN [*d*:][*path*]*original.ext* [*d*:][*path*]*new.ext*

Example: REN OLDFILE.DOC NEWFILE.DOC

TREE

Displays directory paths.

TREE [*d*:][*path*][/F][/A]

Switches:

/F Lists files in each directory.

/A Produces an alternate character for the lines that
link subdirectories. Use for printer output.

Example: TREE /F

TYPE

Displays the contents of a file.

TYPE [*d*:][*path*]*filename.ext* [¦MORE]

Options:

¦MORE Using the MORE filter with the TREE command will cause the output to display one
screen at a time.

Example: TYPE C:\AUTOEXEC.BAT ¦MORE

UNDELETE

Restores deleted files. Also used to establish a delete file tracking system.

```
UNDELETE [d:][path][/LIST][/DT][/DS][/DOS][/
ALL][/PURGE][/LOAD][/UNLOAD][/STATUS][/
S[drive]][/T[drive]]
```

Switches:

/LIST	Lists all files that can be undeleted.
/DT	Uses the tracking file when undeleting.
/DS	Uses the delete sentry file when undeleting.
/DOS	Uses DOS when undeleting.
/ALL	Undeletes without prompting.
/PURGE	Purges the DELETE SENTRY directory.
/LOAD	Loads UNDELETE.
/UNLOAD	Unloads UNDELETE.
/STATUS	Displays status on UNDELETE.
/S	Enables delete sentry.
/T	Enables delete tracking.

Example: UNDELETE \PROGRAMS\JUNK /LIST

145

UNFORMAT

Unformats a diskette.

```
UNFORMAT d: [/P][/L][/TEST]
```

Switches:

/P   Sends output to printer.

/L   Lists files and directories found on disk.

/TEST   Verifies that an UNFORMAT can be done, but doesn't do it.

Example: UNFORMAT A: /TEST

VER

Displays the current DOS version.

```
VER
```

VOL

Displays (and allows you to change) the volume label of a disk.

```
VOL [d:]
```

VSAFE

Loads a memory resident anti-virus program which detects viruses as you work.

```
VSAFE
```

Appendix C
What's New in DOS 6?

This appendix briefly describes the new features and enhancements in DOS 6. See the appropriate lessons for more details.

AUTOEXEC.BAT and CONFIG.SYS

You can define several configuration files and select which one to boot with. You can bypass commands selectively in AUTOEXEC.BAT or CONFIG.SYS, or even boot your computer without them. To completely bypass the AUTOEXEC.BAT and CONFIG.SYS files (clean boot) press F5 at startup. To bypass selected commands in either file, press F8 at startup.

DELTREE

Use the DELTREE command to delete a directory and its subdirectories, *without having to remove its files.* See Lesson 12 for more details.

DoubleSpace

Allows you to compress a disk or diskette so that it will hold up to two times more data. Once DoubleSpace is installed, it works invisibly. See Lesson 20 for more details.

EMM386

Improvements allow EMM386.EXE to take better advantage of unused areas in upper memory. Programs are able to use either expanded or extended memory as needed, without changing your PC's configuration.

Help

On-line Help has been expanded to a complete, graphical, on-line reference to all commands. See Lesson 4 for more details.

Interlink

Provides the ability to link two computers together to transfer files, etc. See Lesson 22 for more details.

MemMaker

MemMaker configures your PC automatically to take best advantage of the memory you have. MemMaker moves device drivers, memory-resident programs, and even DOS out of conventional memory, providing more working memory for all of your programs. See Lesson 21 for more details.

MEM

MEM provides more details about your system's memory usage. Using the /P switch causes MEM to display information one screen at a time. See Lesson 21 for more details.

Microsoft Anti-Virus

DOS now comes with a complete and easy-to-use program for virus detection and removal, based on Central Point's Anti-Virus. There is also an Anti-Virus for Windows. See Lesson 19 for more details.

Microsoft Defragmenter

Based on the Norton Utilities, the Defragmenter can reorganize the files on your PC to allow for faster disk access. If you are not using DoubleSpace, exit all programs (including the DOS Shell and Windows), then type this command to defragment your drive:

```
DEFRAG C:
```

Don't Defrag de Drive   Don't use DEFRAG on a DoubleSpace drive, a network drive, or a drive created by using the INTERLNK command. Also, don't use DEFRAG from a DOS Shell, such as Shell or Windows.

If you have a DoubleSpace drive, use the DoubleSpace utility to defragment it. Select the Tools Defragment command to defragment a DoubleSpace drive.

MOVE

Move files and rename directories with this versatile command. See Lesson 9 for more information.

MSBACKUP

Replacing DOS's antiquated BACKUP program is MSBACKUP, a graphical backup and restore program based on Norton Backup. See Lessons 17 and 18 for more details. A version of MSBACKUP is also provided for Windows.

POWER

Makes better use of your laptop's power. See Lesson 22 for more details.

SMARTDrive

Improvements in writing and reading information allows SMARTDrive to make best use of system resources.

UNDELETE

Provides better tracking and easier recovery of deleted files. There is now an UNDELETE for Windows. See Lesson 10 for more details.

Index

153